CHINESE
IN STEPS

STUDENT BOOK 1

步步高中文1

George X Zhang
Linda M Li
Lik Suen

华语教学出版社·伦敦
Sinolingua · London

Every effort has been made to trace all copyright holders, but if any have been inadvertently overlooked, the publisher will be pleased to make the necessary arrangements at the first opportunity.

Chinese in Steps Series
Chinese in Steps (Student Book 1)
By George X Zhang, Linda M Li, Lik Suen

Editor: Zhang Le, Du Ranran
Cover Design: China-i

This new version, first published and Copyright © 2011 by Sinolingua London Ltd. is published under permission from Cypress Book Co., (UK) Ltd. The original version of Chinese in Steps Volume 1 (ISBN 9781845700027) was published by Cypress Book Co., (UK) Ltd. in 2005.
Second printing in January 2013

Unit 13, Park Royal Metro Centre
Britannia Way
London NW10 7PA
Tel: +44(0)2089519305
Fax: +44(0)2084530709
E-mail: editor@cypressbooks.com
Website: www.sinolingua.com.cn

Distributed by Cypress Book Co., (UK) Ltd.
Tel: +44(0)2084530687
Fax: +44(0)2084530709
E-mail: sales@cypressbooks.com
Website: www.cypressbooks.com

Printed in the People's Republic of China

ISBN 978-1-907838-10-1

About This Series

Chinese in Steps is a series of textbooks designed for English-speaking adults who learn Chinese either as part of their degree study at university, or simply as part of their professional or self-development programme for practical purposes. While aiming to deliver an effective result and an enriching experience of learning Chinese language, it has also taken into consideration the needs of those who seek externally validated qualifications.

Chinese in Steps differs from many other textbooks in its approach to language teaching, and in its conscious effort to make use of adult learners' own rich experiences in learning Chinese. Its approach is based upon how English-speaking adults learning Chinese and aims to deliver language teaching with an integrated method of communicative approach, contrastive analysis and cultural awareness.

Chinese in Steps aims to develop learners' productive communicative competence by focusing on key generic speech patterns and making listening and speaking the core activities of each lesson. The book also aims to develop learners' reading and writing skills with a systematic introduction to relevant knowledge backed up with practice based upon cognitive research, as reading skill is crucial for adult learners to acquire if they expect to use and understand Chinese effectively. The layout of the book is designed to make the contents easy to access and follow. Necessary grammar explanations are given where necessary, but grammatical jargon is kept to a minimum.

Chinese in Steps currently consists of four student's books and one teacher's book. The structure of the student's books, two at Beginners and two at Lower Intermediate levels, is similar, and these two levels are designed to cover most key speech patterns, fundamental grammatical knowledge, 880 frequently used characters, and over 2000 words. By completing the four books, learners should have covered enough ground to be able to cope with many everyday life needs in a Chinese speaking environment and to reach a sound basic B1 level as an independent learner, as proposed by this series with regard to the Common European Framework of Reference. The four books in the series are interconnected and progressive, with the first two books at Beginners level aiming to achieve a basic A2 level. The coming teacher's book will provide practical guide for users of Books 1 and 2. Book 3 continues to build and develop the linguistic and cultural competences of learners while Book 4 consolidates and further cultivates such competences of learners by engaging them in various real tasks in everyday life situations.

Chinese in Steps can be used for university Chinese language programmes or non-credit bearing part-time Chinese language courses for adult learners. In terms of the level attainable, the completion of the first two books will cover enough knowledge and skills to prepare for high GCSE, Intermediate Level in the Asset Language scheme and the initial stages of the Elementary/Intermediate HSK. All the books in the first two stages are accompanied with audio CDs.

Chinese is often perceived as a difficult language in Europe, especially Chinese characters, but its difficulty lies primarily in the fact that it is so different from European languages. It is important to have a *relaxed* and **confident** attitude to the learning of the Chinese language. ***Chinese in Steps*** in many ways endeavours to help learners achieve confidence by gradual introduction to the characteristics of Chinese language as adults learn better and more effectively with a good understanding of what they are doing.

Language skill is acquired over a long period of time and with frequent practice. Learning and revising ***bit by bit*** and practising ***constantly*** and ***frequently*** are keys to success for adult learners who usually find it difficult to devote much time to study. So before you start to learn Chinese, it is important to remain relaxed and confident during the learning process, to enjoy the experience of entering a different linguistic world, and to study and practise gradually and frequently what you learn.

Preface

We are very happy to be able to present this brand new edition of *Chinese in Steps* with Sinolingua London. This is the first new edition of the series since published in 2005 with Cypress Book. We are also most delighted that with the dedication and support from our users, this series was a recent recipient of the Award for Outstanding International Chinese Language Teaching Materials at the Fifth Confucius Institute Conference in December 2010.

Over the last few years, there has been an apparent and rapid growth in the number of people learning Chinese in the UK and around the world. This increase has not only led to a growing demand for quality textbooks, but has also called for the creation of learning and teaching materials that are able to meet the needs and requirements of a variety of students. Whilst we are confident that the content of our series effectively meets such needs, we still adhere to the principle that there is always further room to excel in our future work. We believe that the underlying principles that have guided its compilation and production are sound, based on a thorough understanding of both the needs of our users and how to best meet these needs. This understanding has been constantly enhanced by constructive feedback from our users, to whom we are most grateful. We have tried to incorporate into this latest edition as much feedback as possible so as to make the series even more user-friendly.

There have been some noticeable changes between this and the previous edition. First, real life photos are used in this edition, and we sincerely hope our users like them as it was one of the requests received in user feedback. Second, the number of Chinese characters in each of the first five lessons has increased from 20 to 22, thus bringing them in line with the rest of the book and the subsequent three books. Third, while the Pinyin that accompanies the speech patterns in each lesson has been retained, it is now placed underneath the Chinese sentences so it is less of a distraction for users. Some additional changes include the use of colours and indicators to make the important sections more visual, which was also a suggestion from our users. Besides these changes, the first two books of the series are now accompanied by a Teacher's Book, which we hope will be a useful guide filled with practical tips on using this textbook series.

We feel very fortunate and extremely grateful that so many users of this series, both teachers and students alike, have taken the time and trouble to provide us with their invaluable feedback. What you see in this book is very much the result of this feedback, and we would like to take this opportunity to thank all of our users for their care, consideration and support over all these years. We also sincerely hope that our users will find the changes in this new edition helpful, and will continue to provide their feedback and suggestions for this series.

Finally, we would like to thank Sinolingua London, a specialist publisher of Chinese teaching materials, and Cypress Book, the major distributor of this series, for their unremitting efforts and support in the publication of this new edition. Thanks must also go to all of our colleagues whose work made this new edition possible, especially Managing Director of Sinolingua London, Ms Ru Jing, and editors Ms Zhang Le and Du Ranran.

George X Zhang
Linda M Li
July 2011

语法术语简略表　Abbreviations of Grammatical Terms

adj	adjective
adv	adverb
comp	complement
conj	conjunction
i.e	idiomatic expression
int	interjection
l.w	location word
m.v	modal verb
m.w	measure word
n	noun
num	numeral
o	object
pt	particle
p.n	proper noun
pron	pronoun
prep	preposition
q.w	question word
s	subject
t.w	time word
v	verb
v-c	verb-complement
v-o	verb-object

☻ Chinese characters marked with * are usually not used on their own, but as a component to form another word.

Classroom Expressions 课堂用语：

上课。	Class begins.
下课。	Class is over.
请看黑板。	Please look at the blackboard.
请跟我读。	Please read after me.
请打开书。	Please open your books.
请翻到第5页。	Please turn to Page 5.
请再说一遍。	Please repeat once again.
懂不懂？	Do you understand?
懂了。	Yes, I do.
不懂。	No, I don't.
我们听写。	Let's do a dictation exercise.
请把作业交上来。	Please hand in your homework.
请说得慢一点。	Please speak more slowly.
中文"fish"怎么说。	How do you say fish in Chinese?

目录 Contents

Introduction to Chinese and *Pinyin*

The Official Chinese Language

The official Chinese language is called *Hanyu*. *Hanyu* is also widely used in a number of countries and regions in Southeast Asia, and by numerous Chinese communities all over the world. It is also called *Zhongwen, zhongguohua* and *Huayu*.

Spoken Chinese

China is a large country with many dialects. The official spoken language is called *putonghua* (common speech) — a spoken language primarily based upon the Beijing and northern phonetic system. It is known as "*guoyu*" ("national language") in Taiwan, and Mandarin in the West.

The phonetic systems used to indicate the pronunciations and tones of *putonghua* include *Hanyu pinyin*, *Zhuyinfuhao* and other Romanised phonetic systems. *Hanyu pinyin* is the Romanised alphabetical system used in China's mainland, while *zhuyin* is a system of signs used since 1918 and is still in use in Taiwan. The other romanised systems, such as the Wade-Giles system, are mainly used by Westerners. The UN and other world organizations recognise *Hanyu pinyin* as the official Chinese phonetic system. This book also uses *Hanyu pinyin*.

Chinese Grammar

Chinese is a tonal language that is relatively difficult for Westerners to learn, but Chinese grammar is quite simple compared to that of the English language. Once a character is learned, it will never change its form. There will be no conjugations, declensions, number agreements, case changes etc. to deal with. However, there are a few things that an English speaker should pay special attention to while studying Chinese. These include word formation, particles, measure words, and above all, word order in Chinese sentences.

Chinese Characters

The Chinese written script is Chinese characters. There are about 7,000 characters in modern Chinese. The most frequently used 1,000 characters cover 90% of modern texts; the most frequently used 2,500 characters cover 98.0%; and the most frequently used 3,500 characters cover 99.5%.

There are two kinds of characters—simplified characters and complicated characters (also termed traditional characters). Simplified characters are used in China's mainland, Singapore, official world organisations, and increasingly more in educational institutions in the rest of world, while complicated characters are used in Taiwan, Hong Kong, Macao and many Chinese communities overseas. Transitioning from reading one to the other does not seem to be a significant problem.

Hanyu Pinyin

Hanyu pinyin is a romanised alphabetical system used to indicate the pronunciation of Chinese characters. A character is usually represented by a syllable. Most of the syllables are composed of an initial, a final, and a tone, though some may not have initials. There are 21 initials and 36 finals in Pinyin.

Initials (consonants)

b	p	m	f	d	t	n
l	g	k	h	j	q	x
z	c	s	zh	ch	sh	r

B, p, m, f, d, t, n, i, f, l, h, s are pronounced similarly in Chinese to English. **B, d, g** are unaspirated, while **p, t, k** are aspirated. However, attention should be paid to the following initials:

j	is like	*jee/jea*	as in jeep and jean
q	is like	*chee*	as in cheese and cheek
x	is like	*shee*	as in sheep and sheet
z	is like	*ds*	as in beds or beads
c	is like	*ts*	as in cheats or meets
zh	is like	*dr*	similar to that in drive or dream
ch	is like	*ch*	as in church and match
sh	is like	*sh*	as in English and wish
r			is similar to "r" in English, but with the tip of the tongue curled up slightly more

> **zh-ch-sh** are pronounced with the tip of the tongue curled up slightly.

Finals (all are vowels except those ending with "-n" and "-ng")

Single finals

a	as in	*are*
e	as	*er* (British pronunciation)
i	as the letter	*e*
o	as in	*or*
u	as in	*fool*
ü	as in French	*tu*

Compound finals

It is important to note that compound finals must be pronounced as a single syllable, not separately.

	a	o	e	ai	ei	ao	ou	an	en	ang	eng	ong	er
i	ia		ie			iao	iou (iu)	ian	in	iang	ing	iong	
u	ua	uo		uai	uei (ui)			uan	uen (un)	uang	ueng		
ü			üe					üan	ün				

Tones

Putonghua is a tonal language with four tones; they are: 1st tone, 2nd tone, 3rd tone, 4th tone. They are also known respectively as the high level tone, high rising tone, low falling rising tone and falling tone. There are some syllables that do not have any tonal marks (for example some particle words), and they are called neutral tones.

If we categorize the tone pitches into five groups with 5 as the highest and 1 as the lowest, the following tables illustrate the tones and describe how each tone is pronounced.

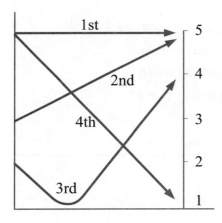

Tone	Mark	Note
1st	*mā*	high level tone （5→5）
2nd	*má*	from a medium to high tone （3→5）
3rd	*mǎ*	from a low medium tone, fall to a low tone and then rise to a high tone （2→1→4）
4th	*mà*	from a high to a low tone （5→1）
neutral	*ma*	a low tone with no variation

拼音总表 Table — Combination of Initials and Finals in *Putonghua* (cont)

Finals / Initials	a	o	e	-i	-i	er	ai	ei	ao	ou	an	en	ang	eng	ong	i	ia	iao	ie
	a	o	e			er	ai	ei	ao	ou	an	en	ang	eng		yi	ya	yao	ye
b	ba	bo					bai	bei	bao		ban	ben	bang	beng		bi		biao	bie
p	pa	po					pai	pei	pao	pou	pan	pen	pang	peng		pi		piao	pie
m	ma	mo	me				mai	mei	mao	mou	man	men	mang	meng		mi		miao	mie
f	fa	fo						fei		fou	fan	fen	fang	feng					
d	da		de				dai	dei	dao	dou	dan	den	dang	deng	dong	di		diao	die
t	ta		te				tai		tao	tou	tan		tang	teng	tong	ti		tiao	tie
n	na		ne				nai	nei	nao	nou	nan	nen	nang	neng	nong	ni		niao	nie
l	la		le				lai	lei	lao	lou	lan		lang	leng	long	li	lia	liao	lie
g	ga		ge				gai	gei	gao	gou	gan	gen	gang	geng	gong				
k	ka		ke				kai	kei	kao	kou	kan	ken	kang	keng	kong				
h	ha		he				hai	hei	hao	hou	han	hen	hang	heng	heng				
j																ji	jia	jiao	jie
q																qi	qia	qiao	qie
x																xi	xia	xiao	xie
z	za		ze	zi			zai	zei	zao	zou	zan	zen	zang	zeng	zong				
c	ca		ce	ci			cai		cao	cou	can	cen	cang	ceng	cong				
s	sa		se	si			sai		sao	sou	san	sen	sang	seng	song				
zh	zha		zhe		zhi		zhai	zhei	zhao	zhou	zhan	zhen	zhang	zheng	zhong				
ch	cha		che		chi		chai		chao	chou	chan	chen	chang	cheng	chong				
sh	sha		she		shi		shai	shei	shao	shou	shan	shen	shang	sheng					
r			re		ri				rao	rou	ran	ren	rang	reng	rong				

Some rules about Pinyin

1. Chinese characters are monosyllabic, so each character corresponds to an existing syllable. Unlike in English, there are no initial consonant clusters such as "st" or "spr" in Chinese, and liaisons are not allowed for two separate syllables; for example *Xī'ān* (two syllables, thus two characters) is completely different from *Xiān* (one character).

2. The *i* in *zi, ci, si, zhi, chi, shi* and *ri* is not pronounced; the sound is like a vocalic extension of the initial consonant. So, the tongue does not move to *i* when pronouncing these sound combinations.

3. The *e* is pronounced differently in *ie* and *üe*. It is like the *e* as in th*e*re.

拼音总表 Table — Combination of Initials and Finals in *Putonghua*

iu	ian	in	iang	ing	iong	u	ua	uo	uai	ui	uan	un	uang	ueng	ü	üe	üan	ün
you	yan	yin	yang	ying	yong	wu	wa	wo	wai	wei	wan	wen	wang	weng	yu	yue	yuan	yun
	bian	bin		bing		bu												
	pian	pin		ping		pu												
miu	mian	min		ming		mu												
						fu												
diu	dian			ding		du		duo		dui	duan	dun						
	tian			ting		tu		tuo		tui	tuan	tun						
niu	nian	nin	niang	ning		nu		nuo			nuan				nü	nüe		
liu	lian	lin	liang	ling		lu		luo			luan	lun			lü	lüe		
						gu	gua	guo	guai	gui	guan	gun	guang					
						ku	kua	kuo	kuai	kui	kuan	kun	kuang					
						hu	hua	huo	huai	hui	huan	hun	huang					
jiu	jian	jin	jiang	jing	jiong										ju	jue	juan	jun
qiu	qian	qin	qiang	qing	qiong										qu	que	quan	qun
xiu	xian	xin	xiang	xing	xiong										xu	xue	xuan	xun
						zu		zuo		zui	zuan	zun						
						cu		cuo		cui	cuan	cun						
						su		suo		sui	suan	sun						
						zhu	zhua	zhuo	zhuai	zhui	zhuan	zhun	zhuang					
						chu	chua	chuo	chuai	chui	chuan	chun	chuang					
						shu	shua	shuo	shuai	shui	shuan	shun	shuang					
						ru	rua	ruo		rui	ruan	run						

4. The compound finals *iou*, *uei*, *uen* are written as *iu*, *ui*, *un* when they form a syllable together with an initial, so they are *liu*, *gui*, *lun* instead of *liou*, *guei*, *luen*.

5. When there are no initials before the final *i*, *u*, *ü* in a syllable, change *i* into *y* or add *y* in front of *i*; change *u* into *w* or add *w* in front of *u*; add *y* in front of *ü* with the two dots over *ü* omitted. There is a rule guiding the change, however. If there is only one vowel in the syllable, one cannot change the syllables but only add to it.

6. The two dots over *ü* are omitted when *ü* appears after *j*, *q* or *x*.

01

第一课   你好！

Learning objectives

Learn and practise the lesson's Pinyin
Learn some useful phrases
Learn the basic numbers, from 0 to 99

 生词 New Words

你	nǐ	*pron*	you
您	nín	*pron*	you (polite form)
我	wǒ	*pron*	I; me
好	hǎo	*adj*	good; well
很	hěn	*adv*	very, rather
不	bù	*adv*	no, not
谢	xiè	*v/n*	thank; Xie (a surname)
客气	kèqi	*adj*	polite, courteous 客 kè guest 气 qì air, weather
再见	zàijiàn	*i.e*	bye, see you again 再 again; later 见 see; meet
吗	ma	*pt*	an interrogative particle
〇	líng	*num*	zero
一	yī	*num*	one
二	èr	*num*	two
三	sān	*num*	three
四	sì	*num*	four
五	wǔ	*num*	five
六	liù	*num*	six
七	qī	*num*	seven
八	bā	*num*	eight
九	jiǔ	*num*	nine
十	shí	*num*	ten

日常用语 Useful Expressions

A: 你好!	Hello!	B: 你好!	Hello!
A: 您好!	How do you do?	B: 您好!	How do you do?
A: 你好吗?	How are you?	B: 我很好。	I'm very well.
A: 谢谢。	Thank you.	B: 不客气。	Not at all.
A: 再见!	Goodbye!	B: 再见!	Goodbye!

数字 Numbers

0	O	líng	11	十一	22	二十二	50	五十
1	一	yī	12	十二	23	二十三	60	六十
2	二	èr	13	十三	24	二十四	70	七十
3	三	sān	14	十四	25	二十五	80	八十
4	四	sì	15	十五	26	二十六	90	九十
5	五	wǔ	16	十六	27	二十七	…	…
6	六	liù	17	十七	28	二十八	95	九十五
7	七	qī	18	十八	29	二十九	96	九十六
8	八	bā	19	十九	30	三十	97	九十七
9	九	jiǔ	20	二十	…	…	98	九十八
10	十	shí	21	二十一	40	四十	99	九十九

文化知识 Cultural Note

中国人的问候 Chinese Greetings

你好 and its more polite form 您好 are common greetings that the Chinese use, and are appropriate for almost any time of the day. There are similar expressions in Chinese for good morning, good afternoon, good evening and good night, but they are not as common. In everyday life, Chinese people use other expressions as greetings.

练习 Exercises

拼音练习 Pinyin Practice

Listen and then repeat after the recording.

1. Tone practice.

1)	mā	má	mǎ	mà
2)	tā	tá	tǎ	tà
3)	zhī	zhí	zhǐ	zhì
4)	jī	jí	jǐ	jì

2. Distinguishing sounds.

1)	sī	shī	2)	cī	chī
3)	cí	chí	4)	jí	qí
5)	zǎo	zhǎo	6)	nǎo	niǎo
7)	lüè	yuè	8)	xiè	jiè

3. Bisyllables.

kāfēi	Ōuzhōu	Bālí	Zhōngguó
zhōngwǔ	hē jiǔ	shāngdiàn	shēngrì
míngtiān	Lúndūn	rénmín	hóngchá

pí jiǔ	niú nǎi	xué yuàn	róng yì
zǒng biān	tǐ cāo	huǎn hé	běn rén
jiǎng yǎn	měi hǎo	yě wài	zhuǎn biàn
Yà zhōu	qì chē	lǜ chá	sì shí
Shàng hǎi	xià xuě	shàng kè	yùn dòng

4. A Chinese Poem—Listen and then read aloud.

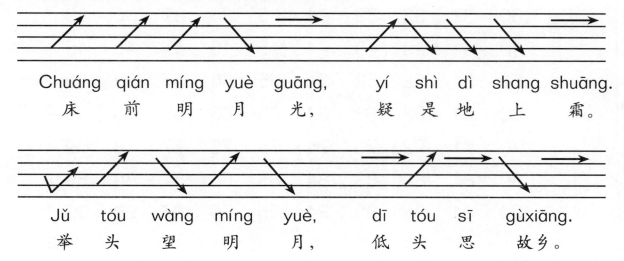

Chuáng qián míng yuè guāng,　yí shì dì shang shuāng.
床　前　明　月　光，　疑　是　地　上　霜。

Jǔ tóu wàng míng yuè,　dī tóu sī gùxiāng.
举　头　望　明　月，　低　头　思　故乡。

听力练习 Listening Practice

1. Listen to the recording and then choose the phrase you have heard in each group.

1)　a. Thank you.　　　b. How are you?　　　c. Hello!
2)　a. Thank you.　　　b. Goodbye!　　　　　c. Not at all.
3)　a. How do you do?　b. I am very well.　　c. Not at all.
4)　a. How are you?　　b. I am very well.　　c. Goodbye!
5)　a. Goodbye!　　　　b. How are you?　　　c. Not at all.
6)　a. Hello!　　　　　b. I am very well.　　c. How are you?

2. Number Game

Please listen to the teacher and then circle the numbers you have heard.

0	1	2	3	4	5	6	7	8	9
10	11	12	13	14	15	16	17	18	19
20	21	22	23	24	25	26	27	28	29
30	31	32	33	34	35	36	37	38	39
40	41	42	43	44	45	46	47	48	49
50	51	52	53	54	55	56	57	58	59
60	61	62	63	64	65	66	67	68	69
70	71	72	73	74	75	76	77	78	79
80	81	82	83	84	85	86	87	88	89
90	91	92	93	94	95	96	97	98	99

认读练习 Matching Exercise

Please follow the example and link each of the Chinese words with their corresponding Pinyin and meanings in English.

再见	nín hǎo	sixteen
你好	zàijiàn	I am very well
十六	bāshíqī	goodbye
你好吗	wǒ hěn hǎo	eighty seven
不客气	nǐ hǎo ma	hello
九十九	bú kèqi	how are you
您好	jiǔshíjiǔ	fifty two
八十七	shíliù	how do you do
我很好	nǐ hǎo	not at all
五十二	wǔshí'èr	ninety nine

汉字知识 Chinese Characters

笔画和笔顺 Strokes and Stroke Order

Chinese characters are made up of strokes, ranging from one stroke to several dozens. Strokes are typically of eight types, most of which appear in the Chinese character for "eternal" (see the Chinese character below left). The eight strokes are respectively explained and presented as below:

点　(diǎn) — a simple dot
横　(héng) — a horizontal stroke from left to right
竖　(shù) — a vertical stroke from top to bottom
折　(zhé) — a bending stroke
提　(tí) — a diagonal stroke from lower left to upper right
勾　(gōu) — a hook usually continued from another stroke
撇　(piě) — a diagonal stroke from upper right to lower left
捺　(nà) — a horizontal stroke, falling from upper left to lower right

When writing Chinese characters, there is an order to follow. The correct **stroke order** in writing Chinese characters follows the five basic rules below:

1) From left to right　　　　　　　　　女 + 子 = 好

2) From top to bottom　　　　　　　　你 + 心 = 您

3) Left-falling strokes precede right-falling strokes　丿 + 乀 = 人

4) Horizontal strokes precede vertical strokes　一 + 丨 = 十

5) Inside strokes precede sealing strokes　四 + 一 = 四

The stroke order of all the new characters covered in this book is illustrated in the relevant lessons, and each Chinese character is presented stroke by stroke in accordance with the above rules.

写字练习 Character Writing Exercise

Can you recognise these characters? Test yourself to see if you are able to write the Pinyin and English meanings above each character. Afterwards, copy each character, following its stroke order. Try to gain a feel for the structure of each character when copying it, especially those consisting of two or three components.

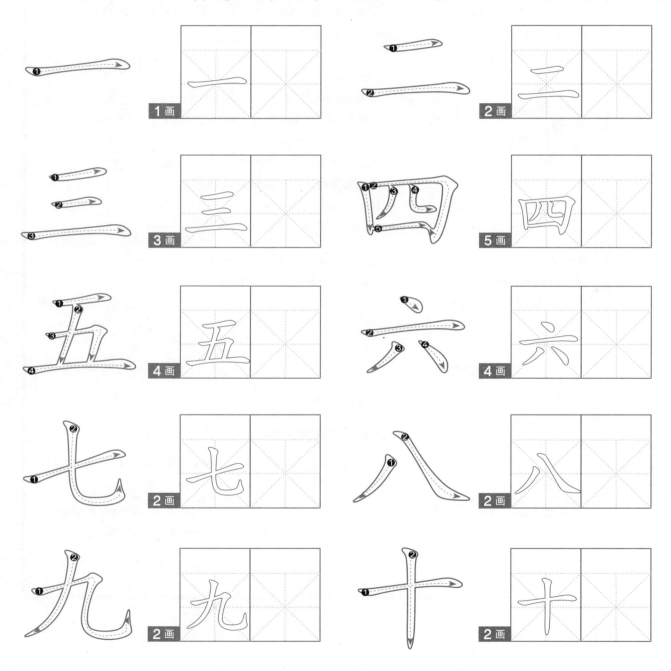

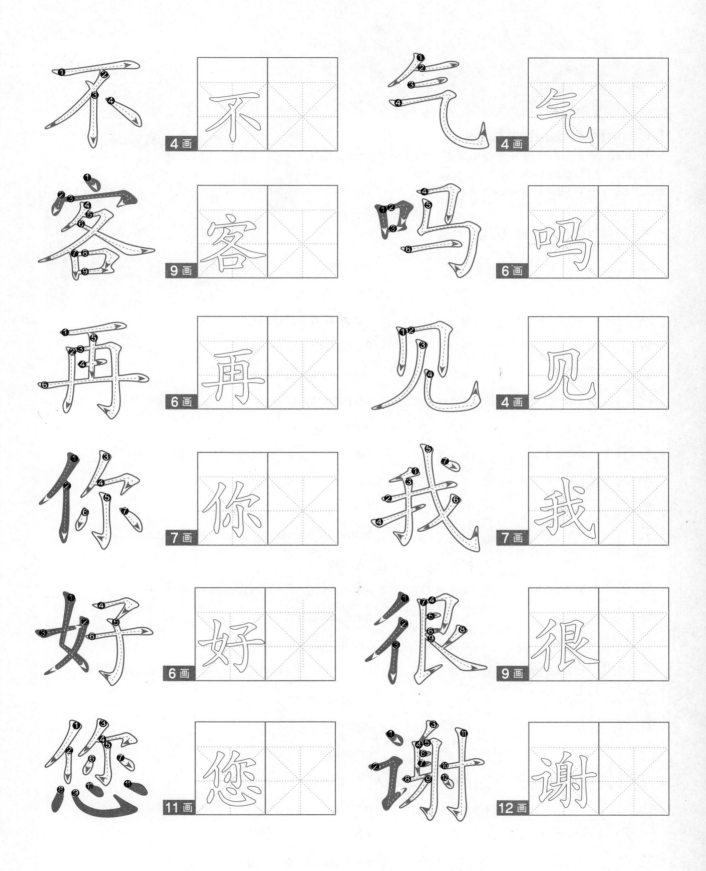

02

第二课   我叫王京

Learning objectives
Introduce yourself to others and ask for others' names
Introduce a third person by his/her name
Practise and revise the lesson's Pinyin

 生词 New Words

他	tā	*pron*	he; him
她	tā	*pron*	she; her
姓	xìng	*v*	have as a surname
叫	jiào	*v*	be called; call; shout
贵	guì	*adj*	honourable; expensive
对	duì	*adj*	correct; right
小	xiǎo	*adj*	small; young
名字	míngzi	*n*	name 名 name 字 zì character
李	Lǐ	*n*	Li (a surname); plum
李贵	Lǐ Guì	*p.n*	Li Gui (a name)
王	Wáng	*n*	Wang (a surname); king
京*	Jīng	*n*	capital
王京	Wáng Jīng	*p.n*	Wang Jing (Jim King) (a name)
英*	yīng	*n*	hero; Britain
李小英	Lǐ Xiǎoyīng	*p.n*	Li Xiaoying (a name)
李月明	Lǐ Yuèmíng	*p.n*	Li Yueming (a name) 月 moon ; month 明 bright
方	fāng	*n*	Fang (a surname); place
国	guó	*n*	country
伦*	lún	*n*	ethics
方国伦	Fāng Guólún	*p.n*	Fang Guolun (a name)
也	yě	*adv*	also, too; neither
什么	shénme	*q.w*	what 什* what 么* what
呢	ne	*pt*	interrogative particle for follow-up questions

句型 Speech Patterns

S	V	N
我 Wǒ	姓 xìng	李。 Lǐ.
他 Tā	叫 jiào	王京。 Wáng Jīng.
她 Tā	叫 jiào	李小英。 Lǐ Xiǎoyīng.

Chinese words do not change forms when used in sentences. There is no verb conjugation in Chinese.

S	V	N	吗
你 Nǐ	姓 xìng	李 Lǐ	吗? ma?
她 Tā	叫 jiào	李小英 Lǐ Xiǎoyīng	吗? ma?
他 Tā	叫 jiào	王京 Wáng Jīng	吗? ma?

A statement can be turned into a general question by adding the question particle 吗 and a question mark to the end of the sentence, and by using a slightly rising tone.

S	Adv	Adv	V	N
我 Wǒ		不 bú	姓 xìng	李。 Lǐ.
他 Tā	也 yě	不 bú	姓 xìng	李。 Lǐ.
她 Tā		不 bú	叫 jiào	王英。 Wáng Yīng.

Adverbs always precede predicate verbs. When 也 and 不 appear in the same statement, 也 will occur before 不 to mean "neither".

S	V	QW
他 Tā	姓 xìng	什么? shénme?
她 Tā	叫 jiào	什么? shénme?
你 Nǐ	叫 jiào	什么（名字）? shénme (míngzi)?

To ask for specific information, simply put the question word in the place where the information would be in the statement, and then add a question mark to the end of the statement.

补充词汇 Additional Vocabulary

Chén	陈	a surname	Bǎoluó	保罗	Paul
Qián	钱	a surname	Dàwèi	大卫	David
Zhāng	张	a surname	Lìsà	莉萨	Lisa
Chéng Lóng	成龙	Jackie Chan	Lùyìsī	路易丝	Louise
Lǐ Xiǎolóng	李小龙	Bruce Lee	Mǎlì	玛丽	Mary
Gǒng Lì	巩俐	Gong Li	Yuēhàn	约翰	John

对话 1 Dialogue One

李：您好！

王：您好！

李：您贵姓[①]？

王：我姓王，我叫王京，您呢[②]？

李：我姓李。

王：您叫李小英吗[③]？

李：对，我叫李小英。

对话 2 Dialogue Two

王：你好！

李：你好！

王：你叫什么名字？

李：我叫李贵。

王：我叫王京。她叫什么名字？

李：她也姓李，她叫李月明。

王：他呢？他也姓李吗？

李：不，他不姓李，他姓方，他叫方国伦。

语法注释 Grammar Notes

① 您贵姓？ — A polite idiomatic expression used to ask someone's family name. It is usually employed on formal occasions when you first meet a person, or when you meet someone who is older or more senior than you. One shouldn't answer it with 贵.

For example:

Question: 您贵姓？
Answer: 我姓李。

② **您呢?** — 呢 is another question particle. Here, it is used to form a follow-up question in a known context without the need to repeat the whole sentence. It is similar to "how about..." or "and you?" in English.

> **For example:**
>
> A: 你好吗?
> B: 我很好，你呢?
> A: 我也很好。

③ **General questions and answers** — For most general questions, you can simply repeat the first verb for "yes", and use 不 plus the first verb for "no". However, for questions that contain such verbs as 姓 and 叫, 对 or 不 should be used to indicate affirmative or negative answers, otherwise full answers should be given.

> **For example:**
>
> Question: 你姓王吗?
> **Affirmative answer:** 对 or 我姓王。
> **Negative answer:** 不 or 我不姓王。

④ While the time word is usually placed before the verb, it can also be placed before the subject. The semantic implication is subtle. The time becomes more salient if it is placed at the beginning of a sentence.

> **For example:**
>
> A: 她今天晚上不看电视。(a statement)
> B: 今天晚上她不看电视。(a statement with emphasis on this evening)

文化知识 Cultural Note

中国人的姓名　Chinese Names

In China, family names always precede given names. Most Chinese family names only have one character, though there are some two-character family names. Typically, Chinese given names have two characters. Traditionally, one of the characters indicates the generation to which one belongs, while the other character reflects the high hopes one's parents place on one. Nowadays however, one-character given names have become very popular.

练习 Exercises

拼音练习 Pinyin Practice

1. Distinguishing tones.

1)	hāo	háo	hǎo	hào
2)	jiān	jián	jiǎn	jiàn
3)	liū	liú	liǔ	liù
4)	zhāng	zháng	zhǎng	zhàng

2. Read the following family names and names.

1)	Sūn	Zhāng	Zhōu	Zhū
2)	Chén	Liú	Táng	Yáng
3)	Kǒng	Mǎ	Lǔ	Lǚ
4)	Fàn	Mèng	Xià	Zhào
5)	Máo Zédōng	Dèng Xiǎopíng	Hú Jǐntāo	Wēn Jiābǎo
6)	Línkěn	Ài yīnsītǎn	Kǎméilún	Àobāmǎ

3. Listen to the recording and then circle the Pinyin you have heard in each group.

1)	jiāo	xiāo	2)	lián	nián
3)	cī	sī	4)	zhāng	chāng
5)	gǎo	kǎo	6)	lán	nán
7)	shī	sī	8)	yuè	yè

听力练习 Listening Practice

Listen to the short dialogues and then mark each of the following sentences as true (T) or false (F).

1. His surname is Li.   (.   )
2. Her name is Wang Jing.   (   )
3. He is not Fang Guolun.   (   )
4. His surname is Bush.   (   )
5. His name is Wang Gui.   (   )
6. His surname is also Wang.   (   )

口语练习 Speaking Practice

1. Introduce yourself in Chinese to another student, and ask what his/her surname and full name is (the names can be said in English).

2. Walk around the class introducing yourself, and find out the full names of at least five of your classmates. Fill these names into the table below, and then report them to the class.

	Family name	Given name
1	李	月明
2		
3		
4		
5		

语法练习 Grammar Practice

1. Rewrite the following sentences in both negative and general question forms.

Example: 我姓李。　　a. 我不姓李。b. 你姓李吗?

1) 我叫李小英。　a. ＿＿＿＿＿　b. ＿＿＿＿＿
2) 我也姓王。　　a. ＿＿＿＿＿　b. ＿＿＿＿＿
3) 他叫方国伦。　a. ＿＿＿＿＿　b. ＿＿＿＿＿
4) 他叫王京。　　a. ＿＿＿＿＿　b. ＿＿＿＿＿
5) 她姓方。　　　a. ＿＿＿＿＿　b. ＿＿＿＿＿
6) 她叫李国英。　a. ＿＿＿＿＿　b. ＿＿＿＿＿

2. Complete the following dialogues by filling in the blanks with the appropriate words given below.

Word list: 姓　什么　也　不　对　呢

1) A: 您贵＿＿＿＿?　　B: 我姓李。

2)　　A: 你叫_____名字?　　　　B: 我叫李月明。

3)　　A: 她姓王吗?　　　　　　　B: _____, 她不姓王。

4)　　A: 我姓李。您贵姓?　　　　B: 我_____姓李。

5)　　A: 我叫方国伦, 你_____?　　B: 我叫李贵。

6)　　A: 他叫王京吗?　　　　　　B: _____, 他叫王京。

认读练习 Matching Exercise

Please follow the example and link each of the Chinese words with their corresponding Pinyin and meanings in English.

贵姓	xiǎomíng	full name
名字	guìxìng	UK
不对	míngzi	your honourable surname
小名	Yīngguó	king
姓名	bú duì	first name
英国	guówáng	not correct
国王	wángguó	pet name for a child
王国	xìngmíng	kingdom
贵国	shénme	what
什么	guìguó	your honourable country

翻译练习 Translation

Say the following sentences in Chinese and then write them out in characters.

1. What's your honourable surname?
2. My name is Wang Ying. What is yours?
3. What's his name?
4. Her surname is also Li.
5. Are you Fang Guolun? No, I am not Fang Guolun.
6. What is your name? I am Fang Ying.

汉字知识 Chinese Characters

汉字的演变 The Evolution of Chinese Characters

Evidence from archaeological discoveries has indicated that Chinese characters date back as far as over 5,000 years ago. These early characters were usually stylised pictures of physical objects presented in horizontal, vertical or curved lines, and etched on pottery or carved on turtle shells and animal bones, bronze utensils, or bamboo slips. The style of writing characrers, however, has undergone a lot of changes over thousands of years of evolution, as illustrated below with the character for horse (*mǎ*). Its current form at the bottom of the page is the simplified character (*jiǎntǐzì*), which has been used since the 1950s.

甲骨文：**jiǎgǔwén**
Oracle bone script
1600 B.C.-1046 B.C.

金文：**jīnwén**
Bronze script
1400 B.C.-220 A.D.

大篆：**dàzhuàn**
Large seal script
1046 B.C.-256 B.C.

小篆：**xiǎozhuàn**
Small seal script
221 B.C.-206 B.C.

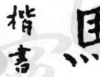

隶书：**lìshū**
Clerical script
206 B.C.-265 A.D.

楷书：**kǎishū**
Regular script
Used since 220 A.D.

行书：**xíngshū**
Running script
Used since 265 A.D.

草书：**cǎoshū**
Cursive script
Used since 48 A.D.

马

简体字：**jiǎntǐzì**
Simplified Chinese
Used since 1950s

写字练习 Character Writing Exercise

Can you recognise these characters? Test yourself to see if you are able to write the Pinyin and English meanings above each character. Afterwards, copy each character, following its stroke order. Try to gain a feel for the structure of each character when copying it, especially those consisting of two or three components.

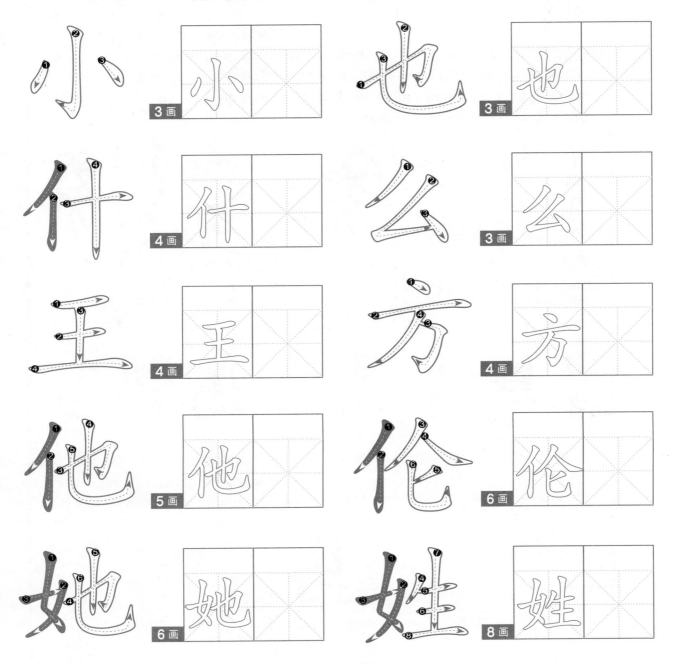

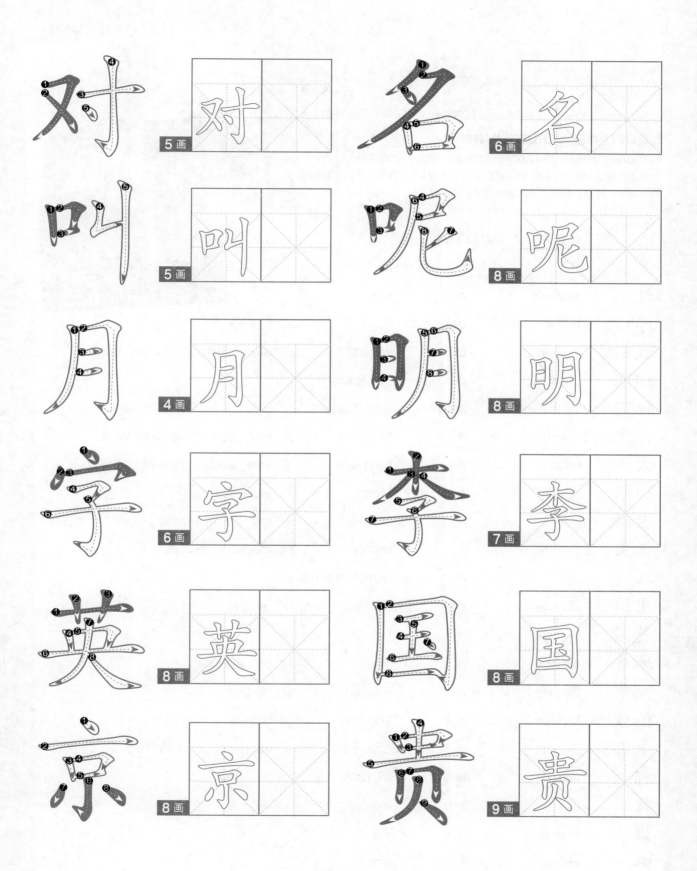

03

第三课   王先生是英国人

Learning objectives

Introduce where you come from and your profession
Ask others for similar details and introduce a third person
Practise and revise the lesson's Pinyin

 生词 New Words

是	shì	*v*	be		
这	zhè/zhèi	*pron*	this		
那	nà/nèi	*pron*	that		
我们	wǒmen	*pron*	we; us	们 *plural suffix for human nouns	
你们	nǐmen	*pron*	you (plural)		
他们	tāmen	*pron*	they; them		
先生	xiānsheng	*n*	Mr; husband	先 first	生 person; to be born
太太	tàitai	*n*	Mrs; wife	太 wife; too (excessively)	
小姐	xiǎojiě	*n*	Miss	姐 elder sister	
老师	lǎoshī	*n*	teacher	老 old	师 master
医生	yīshēng	*n*	doctor	医 medicine; to cure	
人	rén	*n*	person, people		
中国	Zhōngguó	*p.n*	China	中 middle	
英国	Yīngguó	*p.n*	UK		
地方	dìfang	*n*	place	地 place; earth	
北京	Běijīng	*p.n*	Beijing	北 north	
伦敦	Lúndūn	*p.n*	London	敦 *honest	
上海	Shànghǎi	*p.n*	Shanghai	上 above; to go	海 sea
都	dōu	*adv*	all, both		
就	jiù	*adv*	exactly		
谁	shuí/shéi	*q.w*	who		
哪	nǎ/něi	*q.w*	which		

句型 Speech Patterns

S	是	N
这 Zhè	是 shì	李小姐。 Lǐ xiǎojiě .
她 Tā	是 shì	方太太。 Fāng tàitai .
我们 Wǒmen	是 shì	学生。 xuésheng .

The Chinese verb 是 links two "equivalent" parts here, and in this case the word is not stressed. 是 and nouns do not change form no matter whether they are singular or plural.

S	Adv	是	N
他 Tā	不 bú	是 shì	老师。 lǎoshī .
那 Nà	就 jiù	是 shì	王先生。 Wáng xiānsheng .
他们 Tāmen	都 dōu	是 shì	中国人。 Zhōngguórén .

Adverbs, including the negation word 不, emphatic word 就 and inclusive word 都, should be placed before 是 in any sentence structure.

S	是	QW(+N)
你 Nǐ	是 shì	哪国人? nǎ guó rén ?
他 Tā	是 shì	什么地方人? shénme dìfang rén ?
他 Tā	是 shì	谁? shuí ?

As you learned in Lesson 2, Chinese question words can be placed anywhere in a sentence, depending on which piece of information you are asking about.

S	是不是	N
你 Nǐ	是不是 shì bu shì	李英? Lǐ Yīng ?
他 Tā	是不是 shì bu shì	老师? lǎoshī ?
他们 Tāmen	是不是 shì bu shì	中国人? Zhōngguórén ?

An affirmative-negative question is formed with the "verb + not + verb" construction plus a question mark at the end of the sentence. Question particles and question words can't be used in these types of questions.

补充词汇 Additional Vocabulary

Fǎguó	法国	France	gōngchéngshī	工程师	engineer
Bālí	巴黎	Paris	gōngwùyuán	公务员	civil servant
Déguó	德国	Germany	jìzhě	记者	journalist
Bólín	柏林	Berlin	jīnglǐ	经理	manager
Rìběn	日本	Japan	lǜshī	律师	lawyer
Dōngjīng	东京	Tokyo	kuàiji	会计	accountant

 对话 1 Dialogue One

王：您好，我叫王京。

李：您好，我叫李小英。

王：李小姐是哪国人？

李：我是中国人。

王：您是中国什么地方人？

李：我是北京人。

　　王先生是不是英国人①？

王：是，我是伦敦人。

对话 2 Dialogue Two

方：王老师，这是李小姐。

　　李小姐，这是王老师。

李：您好，王老师。

王：你好，李小姐。

方：王老师，李小姐也是上海人。

王：是吗？我们②都③是上海人。

方：那是谁？那是不是您太太？

王：是，那就是我太太④。

李：王太太也是老师吗？

王：不，她是医生。

语法注释 Grammar Notes

① **Answering an affirmative-negative question**
—simply use the verb for "yes" or 不 plus the verb for "no".

For example:

Question: 你是不是中国人？
Affirmative answer: 是。
Negative answer: 不是。

② 们 —This makes pronouns plural when it is added to them, such as 我们, 你们, 他们 and 她们. However, while this suffix can be added to nouns addressing to a group of people such as 老师们, it can't be used for animals, or groups of people that have numeral modifiers before them.

③ 都 —都 refers to two or more nouns, equaling to "both" and "all" in English. It is an adverb, and never procedes a noun or pronoun. When it is used with 不, the position of 都 (before or after 不) will affect the meaning of a sentence.

> **For example:**
>
> 我们都不是老师。
> **None of us is a teacher. (total negation)**
> 我们不都是老师。
> **Not all of us are teachers. (partial negation)**

④ 那就是我太太 —就 is here for emphasis, meaning "precisely" or "exactly". For example, when someone who doesn't know you is looking for you and calling out your name, you can step forward and say, 我就是.

文化知识　Cultural Note

中国人的称谓　How the Chinese address each other

As a mark of respect, the Chinese usually address each other by their professional or official title, which is attached as a suffix to the family name. This is why you may often hear 李老师 (Teacher Li), 王医生 (Doctor Wang), and so on. Other common titles include 先生, 太太, and 小姐, which can be used as formal but general terms of address when one is unsure of the other's position or profession. Those who know each other well will add the prefix 老 or 小 before the family name to form an informal term of address; e.g., 老李, 小王. The choice of prefix is generally age related. Given names are usually used among family members, close friends, classmates and colleagues.

练习 Exercises

 ### 拼音练习 Pinyin Practice

1. Distinguishing sounds.

1)	yā	yē	yāng	yōu
2)	qié	qiáo	qiú	qué
3)	shǎn	shǎng	shěn	shěng
4)	rè	ruò	rào	ròu

2. Read the following city and country names.

1)	Tiānjīn	Kūnmíng	Xiānggǎng (HK)	Lāsà
2)	Wúxī	Héféi	Táiběi	Chóngqìng
3)	Guǎngzhōu	Jǐnán	Hǎikǒu	Wǔhàn
4)	Guìzhōu	Dàlián	Shànghǎi	Dàqìng
5)	Xībānyá (Spain)	Hélán (Holland)	Mǎdélǐ (Madrid)	Ài'ěrlán (Ireland)
6)	Nuówēi (Norway)	Éluósī (Russia)	Bǐlìshí (Belgium)	Mòsīkē (Moscow)

3. Listen to the recording and then circle the Pinyin you have heard in each group.

1)	chāng	shāng	2)	jiǔ	zǒu
3)	chù	qù	4)	xiàn	shàn
5)	jué	qué	6)	lǜ	lù
7)	róng	lóng	8)	luǎn	nuǎn

  ### 听力练习 Listening Practice

Listen to the short dialogues and then mark each of the following sentences as true (T) or false (F).

1. Her surname is Li.   (   )
2. Teacher Xie is French.   (   )
3. Mr Wang is from London.   (   )
4. Mrs Wang is a doctor.   (   )
5. Miss Fang is not from Britain.   (   )
6. Not all of them are Chinese.   (   )

口语练习 **Speaking Practice**

1. Work in pairs or small groups to introduce to each other who you are and where you are from.

2. Please introduce to others someone you know who belongs to one of the following professions.

Family name	Given name	Profession	Country	City
		yīshēng (*doctor*)		
		lǎoshī (*teacher*)		
		lùshī (*lawyer*)		
		gōngchéngshī (*engineer*)		
		jīnglǐ (*manager*)		

语法练习 **Grammar Practice**

1. Turn the following sentences into choice questions (CQ) or special questions (SQ), based on the underlined words.

| **Example:** | 我是<u>英国</u>人。 | 你是哪国人？ | (SQ) |
| | | 你是不是英国人？ | (CQ) |

1) 他叫<u>李贵</u>。 _____ (SQ)

2) 我姓<u>王</u>。 _____ (SQ)

3) 王小姐是<u>伦敦</u>人。 _____ (SQ)

4) 他们的老师是<u>中国</u>人。 _____ (CQ)

5) 那是<u>方小姐</u>。 _____ (SQ)

6) 我们是<u>医生</u>。 _____ (CQ)

2. Complete the following dialogues by filling in the blanks with the appropriate words given below.

Word list: 哪 什么 都 不 谁 不是

1)　A: 你是_____国人?　　　　　B: 我是英国人。

2)　A: 他是_____?　　　　　　　B: 他是方老师。

3)　A: 你们是_____是伦敦人?　　B: 我们是伦敦人。

4)　A: 她是_____地方人?　　　　B: 她是上海人。

5)　A: 你们都是中国人吗?　　　　B: 我们不_____是中国人。

6)　A: 他是不是医生?　　　　　　B: _____, 他是老师。

认读练习 Matching Exercise

Please follow the example and link each of the Chinese words with their corresponding Pinyin and meanings in English.

中医	míngrén	old people
生字	rénmíng	northerner
生人	shēngrén	new character
老人	běifāngrén	name of a person
名人	zhōngyī	north
人名	lǎorén	Chinese medicine
北方	shēngzì	famous people
北方人	běifāng	stranger
姐姐	zhōngyī yīshēng	doctor of traditional Chinese medicine
中医医生	jiějie	elder sister

翻译练习 Translation

Say the following sentences in Chinese and then write them out in characters.

1. Which country are you from?
2. Who is he? He is the very person — Teacher Wang.
3. This is Miss Fang. She is also from Beijing.
4. That is Mr Li. He is a doctor.
5. We are all British.
6. None of them are doctors.

 汉字知识 Chinese Characters

象形字 Pictographic Characters

A pictograph is a graphic depiction of a physical object. Most early Chinese characters discovered through archaeological findings were like "pictures" of objects. Characters in the middle column of the table below are a result of long years of evolution of the respective pictographs in the left column. Can you guess the English meanings for each Chinese character and then write it down in the column on the right?

Pictographs and their evolution	Character	English meaning
☉ ☉ ⊖ ⊟	日 rì	
☽ ☽ ☽ ☽	月 yuè	
⛰ ⛰ 山	山 shān	
〜 巛 巛	水 shuǐ	
🐦 🐦 🐦	鸟 niǎo	

写字练习 Character Writing Exercise

Can you recognise these characters? Test yourself to see if you are able to write the Pinyin and English meanings above each character. Afterwards, copy each character, following its stroke order. Try to gain a feel for the structure of each character when copying it, especially those consisting of two or three components.

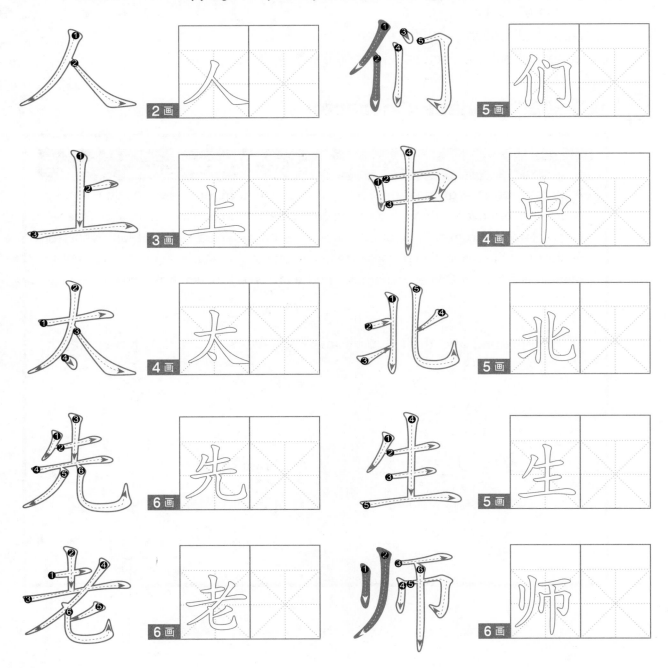

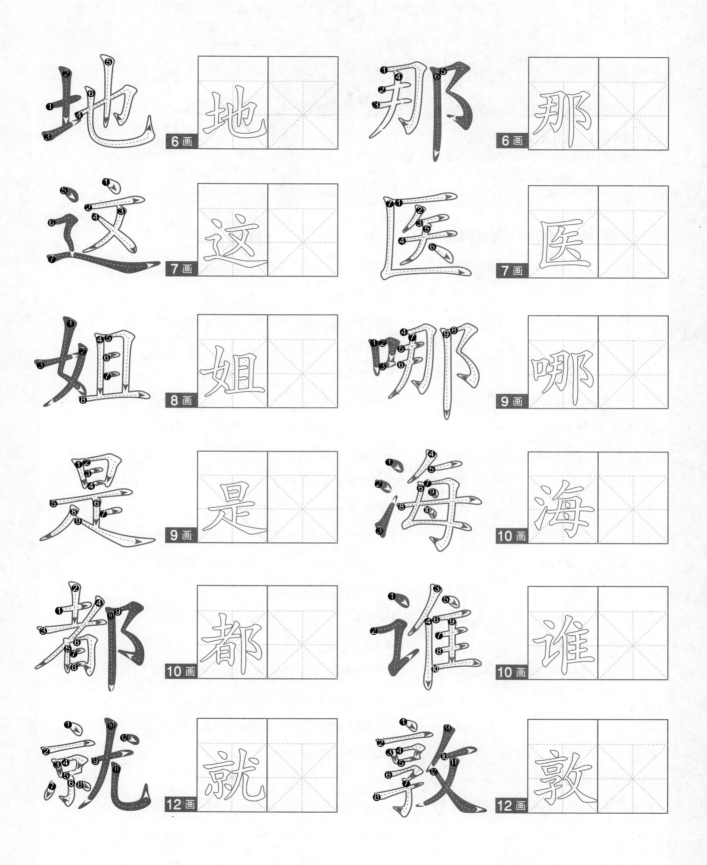

04

第四课　　今天几号？

Learning objectives
Be able to state and ask the date, month and day of the week
Talk and ask about someone's age and birthday
Practise and revise the lesson's Pinyin

🔊 生词 New Words

今天	jīntiān	*t.w*	today	今* today; this　　天 day; sky
明天	míngtiān	*t.w*	tomorrow	
后天	hòutiān	*t.w*	the day after tomorrow	后 behind, after
今年	jīnnián	*t.w*	this year	年 year
九月	jiǔyuè	*t.w*	September	
十一月	shíyīyuè	*t.w*	November	
星期	xīngqī	*n*	week	星 star　　期 period
星期二	xīngqī'èr	*t.w*	Tuesday	
生日	shēngrì	*n*	birthday	日 day (formal); sun
号	hào	*n*	date; number; size	
弟弟	dìdi	*n*	younger brother	弟 younger brother
妹妹	mèimei	*n*	younger sister	妹 younger sister
岁	suì	*m.w/n*	year (age); time	
快乐	kuàilè	*adj*	happy	快 pleased　　乐 happy
大	dà	*adj*	big; old (age)	
几	jǐ	*q.w*	how many (used for less than 10)	
多	duō	*q.w/adj*	how many/much; many, much	
的	de	*pt*	an attributive and possessive particle	
吧	ba	*pt*	an interrogative or suggestive particle	
年纪	niánjì	*n*	age	纪* age; record
对不起	duìbuqǐ	*i.e*	sorry, pardon, excuse me	起* rise
知道	zhīdào	*v*	know	知 know　　道 way, method

🔘 句型　Speech Patterns

S	Adv	是	Day/Date
今天 Jīntiān		(是) shì	二号。 èr hào .
今天 Jīntiān	不 bú	是 shì	星期天。 xīngqītiān .
明天 Míngtiān	不 bú	是 shì	九月十号。 jiǔyuè shí hào .

The verb 是 is often omitted when talking about the time and date in Chinese, especially in spoken Chinese. But 是 cannot be omitted when the adverb 不, 也 or 都 is in the sentence.

S	是	Day/Date
今天 Jīntiān	(是) shì	几号? jǐ hào ?
今天 Jīntiān	(是) shì	星期几? xīngqī jǐ ?
明天 Míngtiān	(是) shì	几月几号? jǐ yuè jǐ hào ?

The special question word 几, not 什么, is used to ask about days and dates because the answers are numbers.

S	TW	Adv	是	Num 岁
我弟弟 Wǒ dìdi				九岁。 jiǔ suì .
我姐姐 Wǒ jiějie	今年 jīnnián			二十岁。 èrshí suì .
我 Wǒ	今年 jīnnián	不 bú	是 shì	十八岁。 shíbā suì .

As seen in the first speech pattern, when talking about age, the verb 是 is usually omitted, but it cannot be omitted when 不 is present.

S	TW	QW	N
你弟弟 Nǐ dìdi	今年 jīnnián	几 jǐ	岁? suì ?
你姐姐 Nǐ jiějie		多大? duō dà ?	
方老师 Fāng lǎoshī		多大 duō dà	年纪? niánjì ?

When asking about age, 几岁 is usually used for children, while 多大 is used for adults. 多大年纪 is a way to ask about the age of someone who appears to be of middle age or older.

🔘 补充词汇　Additional Vocabulary

Days of the week: 星期 + number (except Sunday)						
星期一	星期二	星期三	星期四	星期五	星期六	星期日／天
Months of the year: number + 月						
一月	二月	三月	四月	五月	六月	
七月	八月	九月	十月	十一月	十二月	

对话 1 Dialogue One

李：王京，今天星期几？

王：今天星期二。

李：今天几号？

王：二十三号。

李：九月二十三号！

明天是我弟弟的^①生日。

王：是吗？他今年几岁？

李：他今天八岁，明天九岁。

王：我妹妹今年也九岁。

李：她的生日是哪天^②？

王：十一月七号。

对话 2 Dialogue Two

王：李英，你的生日是几月几号？

李：11月14号。

王：11月14号？后天就是11月14号吧^③？

李：对。后天就是我的生日。

王：生日快乐！

李：谢谢。

王：你今年多大？

李：我今年20岁。你的生日是哪天？

王：5月6号^④。

李：5月6号也是方老师的生日。

王：方老师今年多大年纪？

李：对不起，我不知道。

语法注释 Grammar Notes

① **Attributive/Possessive marker 的** —的 can be used to indicate a possessive relationship between two parts, like "David's" in English. When the relationship is closely personal, and the "owner" is in the form of a pronoun, this marker is often omitted.

> **For example:**
>
> 方先生是王京的老师。
> Mr Fang is Jim King's teacher.
> 李英是我姐姐。
> Li Ying is my elder sister.

② **她的生日是哪天?** —哪天 is similar in meaning to几月几号, and it is more colloquial.

③ **后天就是11月14号吧?** — 吧 is a particle that accompanies suggestions or suppositions. Here it is used to indicate that the speaker expects confirmation from the listener. If the suggestion or supposition is less certain, 吗 is used instead.

> **For example:**
>
> 明天是五号吧?
> Tomorrow is the 5th, isn't it?
> 明天是五号吗? Is tomorrow the 5th?

④ **日/号 and 日/天** —号 and 日 are both used to refer to dates. 号 is more colloquial, while 日 is more formal. Similarly, 星期天 is more colloquial than 星期日, and thus is used more often in everyday life.

⑤ **The order for expressing dates and days of the week in Chinese** — Dates in Chinese start with the largest unit (year) and end with the smallest unit (day). While the month and date can be written in Arabic numerals, the numerals that indicate the day of the week are never written that way.

English	Chinese	
05/09	9月5日	九月五日
10/1914	1914年10月	一九一四年十月
1966	1966年	一九六六年

English	Chinese	
28/04/1935	1935年4月28日	一九三五年四月二十八日
Fri.05/08/2011	2011年8月5日星期五	二0一一年八月五日星期五

文化知识 Cultural Note

中国人看数字 Chinese Numbers

As in all other cultures, the numbers 1 to 9 have cultural connotations in Chinese. For instance, the Chinese regard 6 and 8 as lucky numbers, as 6 signifies "smooth" and 8 rhymes with the word "become rich" (*fā*). 4 is regarded as an unlucky number because it sounds similar to the word "death" (*sǐ*). 9 is a magic and powerful number, as it is the highest amongst the single digit numbers. It has the same meaning of "many" as it does in English.

练习 Exercises

拼音练习 Pinyin Practice

1. Distinguishing sounds.

1)	sūn	suān	sān	sāng
2)	chóng	chóu	chún	cháo
3)	lǎo	liǎo	lǒu	luǒ
4)	zuì	zài	zàn	zuàn

2. Read the following professions and titles.

1)	gōngrén	(worker)	nóngmín	(peasant)
2)	yǎnyuán	(actor/actress)	hùshi	(nurse)

3)	kēxuéjiā	(scientist)	shùxuéjiā	(mathematician)
4)	shòuhuòyuán	(salesperson)	fúwùyuán	(waiter/waitress)
5)	xiàozhǎng	(head of a school)	chǎngzhǎng	(head of a factory)
6)	dǒngshìzhǎng	(chairperson of the board)	zǒngtǒng	(president of a state)

3. Listen to the recording and then circle the Pinyin you have heard in each group.

1)	jīn	qīn	2)	xīn	yīn
3)	róu	lóu	4)	yóu	móu
5)	liǎo	niǎo	6)	miǎo	xiǎo
7)	cùn	xùn	8)	jùn	hùn

听力练习 Listening Practice

1. Listen to the short dialogues and then choose the correct answer for each question.

1)	a. 十月一号	b. 十月十一号	c. 十一月一号
2)	a. 二月二十一日	b. 十二月七日	c. 二月十七日
3)	a. 星期一	b. 星期二	c. 星期三
4)	a. 英国人	b. 伦敦人	c. 中国人
5)	a. 六月二十九号	b. 六月九号	c. 九月六号
6)	a. 我姐姐的	b. 我妹妹的	c. 我弟弟的

口语练习 Speaking Practice

1. Working in pairs, ask each other questions about the days and dates for today and tomorrow.

2. The following dates are the birthdays of people you know. Please tell the other students a bit more about them (their name, age, profession, nationality, etc.) ?

1)	14 Jan. 1955	2)	29 Mar. 1983
3)	31 July 1978	4)	28 Nov. 2004

语法练习 Grammar Practice

1. Ask questions about the underlined parts in the following sentences.

> **Example:**　她的生日是明天。　她的生日是哪天?

1)　我的生日是九月十五号。　2)　我妹妹今年十岁。

3)　今天星期六，明天星期天。　4)　后天是李老师的生日。

5)　星期三是小李的生日。　6)　王老师是中国北京人。

2. Complete the following dialogues by filling in the blanks with the appropriate words given below.

> **Word list:**　多　的　几　三月六号　明天　几岁

1)　A: 你的生日是几月几号?　　B: 我的生日是_____。

2)　A: 你弟弟今年_____?　　B: 八岁。

3)　A: 明天是你_____生日吗?　　B: 不是。

4)　A: 她_____大?　　B: 她今年十九岁。

5)　A: 今天六号。　　B: _____七号。

6)　A: 今天星期_____?　　B: 对不起，我不知道。

认读练习 Matching Exercise

Please follow the example and link each of the Chinese words with their corresponding Pinyin and meanings in English.

年年	míngxīng	elderly people
明月	suìyuè	time
明星	zhōngniánrén	everyone
老年人	míngyuè	medium size
中年人	niánnián	star (celebrity)
大号	lǎoniánrén	middle-aged people
小号	dàhào	bright moon
岁月	rénrén	every year
人人	zhōnghào	large size
中号	xiǎohào	small size

翻译练习 Translation

Say the following sentences in Chinese and then write them out in characters.

1. What's the date today?
2. Today is your birthday. Happy birthday!
3. How old are you?
4. It is 2011 this year. Next year is 2012.
5. What day is it tomorrow? It is Saturday tomorrow.
6. Who is he? He is my younger sister's teacher.

 ## 汉字知识 Chinese Characters

指事字 Indicative Characters

Indicative characters make use of indicative signs to refer to implied ideas. Compared to pictographic characters, they are more abstract and symbolic.

There are two types of indicatives. One is composed of a pictograph and an indicating sign. For example, the character for knife and its derivative for knife edge.

Pictograph　　　　　　　　　　　　　　　　　**Indicative**

刀　　add an indicative **dot** near the edge of the knife to refer to the edge, thus　　刃

dāo knife　　　　　　　　　　　　　　　　　*rèn* knife edge

The other type of indicative is constructed purely from abstract strokes to indicate a meaning. For example, 一 , 二 and 三 are used to indicate one, two, and three. A slightly more abstract pair of indicatives are positional words, which are shown below.

上　　flipped upside down　　下

shàng above　　　　　　　　　　　　　　*xià* below

写字练习 Character Writing Exercise

Can you recognise these characters? Test yourself to see if you are able to write the Pinyin and English meanings above each character. Afterwards, copy each character, following its stroke order. Try to gain a feel for the structure of each character when copying it, especially those consisting of two or three components.

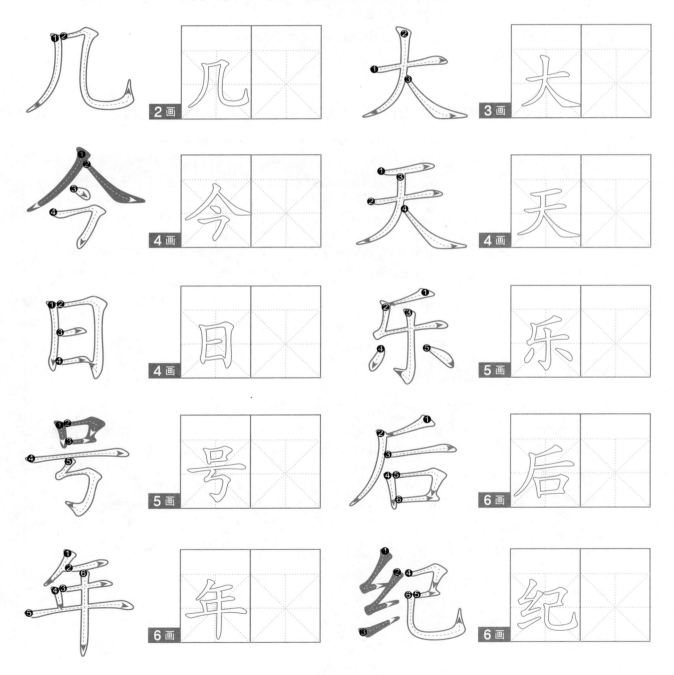

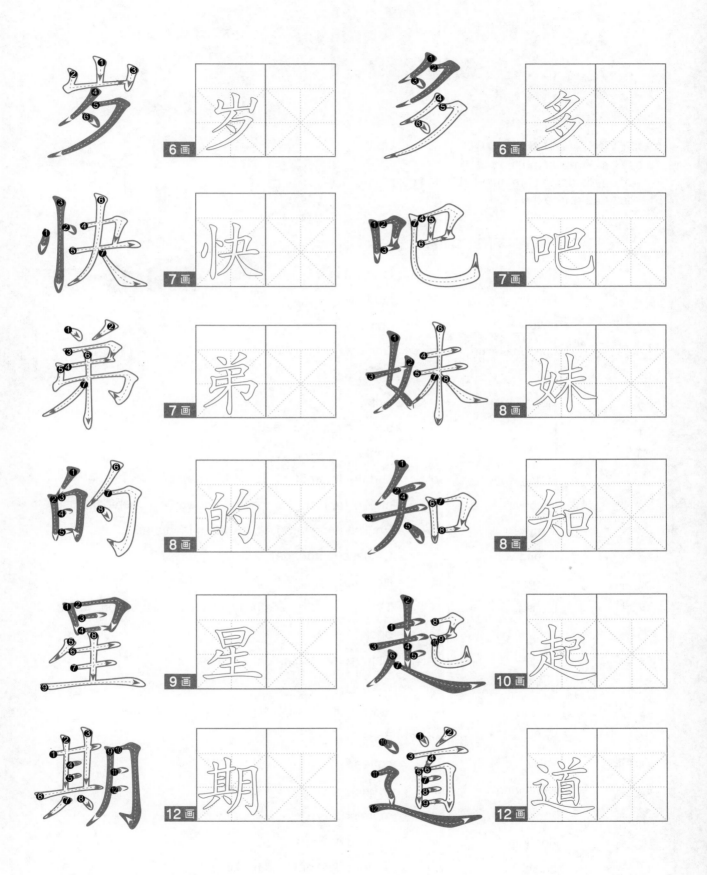

05

第五课   他天天晚上都写汉字

Learning objectives

To say one does something
To say one is doing something at a particular time
Practise and revise the lesson's Pinyin

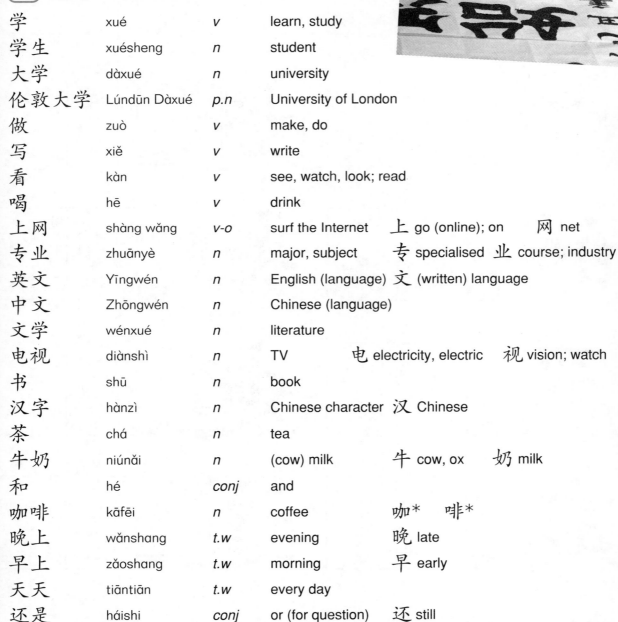

生词 New Words

学	xué	*v*	learn, study
学生	xuésheng	*n*	student
大学	dàxué	*n*	university
伦敦大学	Lúndūn Dàxué	*p.n*	University of London
做	zuò	*v*	make, do
写	xiě	*v*	write
看	kàn	*v*	see, watch, look; read
喝	hē	*v*	drink
上网	shàng wǎng	*v-o*	surf the Internet 上 go (online); on 网 net
专业	zhuānyè	*n*	major, subject 专 specialised 业 course; industry
英文	Yīngwén	*n*	English (language) 文 (written) language
中文	Zhōngwén	*n*	Chinese (language)
文学	wénxué	*n*	literature
电视	diànshì	*n*	TV 电 electricity, electric 视 vision; watch
书	shū	*n*	book
汉字	hànzì	*n*	Chinese character 汉 Chinese
茶	chá	*n*	tea
牛奶	niúnǎi	*n*	(cow) milk 牛 cow, ox 奶 milk
和	hé	*conj*	and
咖啡	kāfēi	*n*	coffee 咖* 啡*
晚上	wǎnshang	*t.w*	evening 晚 late
早上	zǎoshang	*t.w*	morning 早 early
天天	tiāntiān	*t.w*	every day
还是	háishi	*conj*	or (for question) 还 still

句型 Speech Patterns

S	V	O
我 Wǒ	学 xué	中文。 Zhōngwén.
你 Nǐ	看 kàn	书。 shū.
我们 Wǒmen	上 shàng	网。 wǎng.

> For sentences with action verbs, Chinese has the same S-V-O sentence order as English.

S	TW	Adv	V	O
我 Wǒ	晚上 wǎnshang		写 xiě	汉字。 hànzì.
你们 Nǐmen	天天 tiāntiān	都 dōu	上 shàng	网。 wǎng.
她 Tā	明天 míngtiān	不 bú	看 kàn	电视。 diànshì.

> It is important to remember that the time word always goes before a verb. But time words can also be placed before the subject to emphasise the time. For example, 明天她不看电视.

S	TW	Adv	V	O
你 Nǐ	今天晚上 jīntiān wǎnshang		写 xiě	什么？ shénme?
你们 Nǐmen	天天 tiāntiān	都 dōu	做 zuò	什么？ shénme?
谁 Shuí	明天晚上 míngtiān wǎnshang	不 bú	看 kàn	电视？ diànshì?

> To ask who is doing what, simply use an appropriate question word to replace the relevant part of the speech pattern and add a question mark to the end of the sentence.

S	V	O1	还是	V	O2
他 Tā	是 shì	老师 lǎoshī	还是 háishi		医生？ yīshēng?
你 Nǐ	喝 hē	茶 chá	还是 háishi	(喝) (hē)	咖啡？ kāfēi?
他 Tā	看 kàn	书 shū	还是 háishi	上 shàng	网？ wǎng?

> 还是 here links two choices to form an alternative question. Unlike the English "or", 还是 is usually used in questions, not in statements. If the second verb is the same as the first, it is usually omitted.

补充词汇 Additional Vocabulary

Fǎwén	法文	French	zuò fàn	做饭	cook (a meal)
Déwén	德文	German	chī fàn	吃饭	eat
Rìwén	日文	Japanese	jiǔ	酒	alcoholic drink
kàn diànyǐng	看电影	watch films	kělè	可乐	cola
kàn xiǎoshuō	看小说	read novels	guǒzhī	果汁	fruit juice
zuò zuòyè	做作业	do homework	kuàngquánshuǐ	矿泉水	mineral water

对话 1 Dialogue One

方：你好，我叫方京。

李：你好，我叫李英。

方：你是学生吗？

李：对，我是伦敦大学的学生。

方：你学什么专业？

李：我学中文。你呢？

方：我学英国文学。
你今天晚上做什么？

李：我写汉字。

方：你明天晚上做什么？

李：我写汉字。

方：你天天晚上都写汉字吗？[①]

李：对。你晚上都做什么？[②]

方：我看书、看电视、上网。

对话 2 Dialogue Two

李：小王，你喝不喝茶？

王：我早上不喝，谢谢。

李：你早上喝什么？

王：我喝牛奶和咖啡。你喝咖啡吗？

李：我不喝咖啡，早上晚上我都喝茶。

王：你喝中国茶还是英国茶？

李：我喝中国茶。

语法注释 Grammar Notes

① 你天天晚上都写汉字吗？ — 都 is used here to emphasise "every evening". Since 天天晚上都 are all adverbial words, you have to put them before the verb 写. However you can't put 都 before 天天晚上 as 都 normally modifies the word before it.

② 你晚上都做什么？ — Here the speaker wants to know everthing you do in the evening. They expect to have things listed in your reply. However, 都 cannot be used in your reply unless you place the objects before the verb.

For example:

A: 你都喝什么？
B: 我喝牛奶，也喝英国茶。
   or 牛奶、英国茶我都喝。

③ 她明天不看电视 — The negation 不 in this sentence should be used after the time word. However, if the time word is of a non-specific nature such as 天天, 不 can be used before or after the time word to indicate partial negation and total negation respectively. While 都 is needed for a total negation, it is optional in a partial negation.

For example:

Compare: 她今天不写汉字。
她不(=不是)天天都写汉字。
她天天都不写汉字。

④ While the time word is usually placed before the verb; it can also be placed before the subject. The semantic implication is subtle, and the time becomes more salient if it is placed at the beginning of a sentence.

For example:

A: 她今天晚上不看电视。 a statement
B: 今天晚上她不看电视。 a statement with emphasis on this evening

文化知识 Cultural Note

中文的语序 Word Order in Chinese

Unlike in English, time words in Chinese must be placed before the verb. This is also true of place nouns, as you will soon learn. This difference reflects how the two languages perceive an action. The English language focuses on actions or status, so time and place are normally placed after verbs in sentences. By contrast, the Chinese language tends to emphasise the process of actions or status, so time and place precede verbs in sentences as they are important conditions for actions or status to be achieved. For example, 我天天晚上写汉字.

练习 Exercises

拼音练习 Pinyin Practice

1. Distinguishing sounds.

1) jiǔ   jiǎo   jiǎ   jiě

2) shēn   shān   shuān   shuāng

3) zuǒ   zǒu   suǒ   sǒu

4) chuò   cuò   suò   shuò

2. Read the following names of public places.

1) chāoshì   (supermarket)   yóujú   (post office)

2) jiǔbā   (bar)   fànguǎnr   (restaurant)

3) fēijīchǎng   (airport)   túshūguǎn   (library)

4) tíngchēchǎng   (car park)   bówùguǎn   (museum)

5) huǒchēzhàn   (train station)   měiróngyuàn   (beauty salon)

6) yuèlǎnshì   (reading room)   diànyǐngyuàn   (cinema)

3. Listen and circle the Pinyin you have heard in each group.

1) dìtú   dìtóu   2) diàotóu   dàlóu

3) sānshí   sàngshī   4) shǒushì   shuòshì

5) chángzhēng   Chángchéng   6) chánghóng   chánglóng

7) jiǎn fà   jiěfàng   8) jiǎnhuà   jiǎng huà

听力练习 Listening Practice

Listen to the short dialogues and then mark each of the following sentences as true (T) or false (F).

1. She studies Chinese.   (   )

2. She will watch TV tonight.   (   )

3. Li Ying's major is English literature.   (   )

4. Wang Jing studies Chinese on Sunday evenings.   (   )

5. She drinks milk in the morning.   (   )

6. She writes characters in the morning.   (   )

口语练习　Speaking Practice

1. Following the example, work in pairs to find out what each other does each day of the week. You may use English in your answers.

Q: 你星期一早上做什么？　　**A:** 我星期一早上 go to work。

Q: 你星期一晚上做什么？　　**A:** 我星期一晚上看电视。

星期	早上	晚上
星期一		
星期二		
星期三		
星期四		
星期五		
星期六		
星期日		

2. Work in pairs and find out what each other drinks during the day.

语法练习　Grammar Practice

1. Please place the words provided in brackets in the correct place in each sentence.

Example:　她不喝英国茶。（早上）　她早上不喝英国茶。

1) 英国人喝英国茶吗？ （都）

2) 你看电视吗？ （今天晚上）

3) 她上网。 （天天）

4) 我们学英国文学。 （不）

5) 他不喝中国茶，我不喝中国茶。 （也）

6) 这是谁茶？ （的）

2. Complete the following dialogues by filling in the blanks with the appropriate words given below.

Word list: 还是 写 中文 喝 都 上网

1) A: 你学什么专业？ B: 我学_____。

2) A: 你晚上_____做什么？ B: 上网、看电视。

3) A: 你明天晚上做什么？ B: 我_____汉字。

4) A: 你看中文书_____看英文书？ B: 我看英文书。

5) A: 你早上喝牛奶吗？ B: _____。

6) A: 你晚上_____吗？ B: 不上。

认读练习 Matching Exercise

Please follow the example and link each of the Chinese words with their corresponding Pinyin and meanings in English.

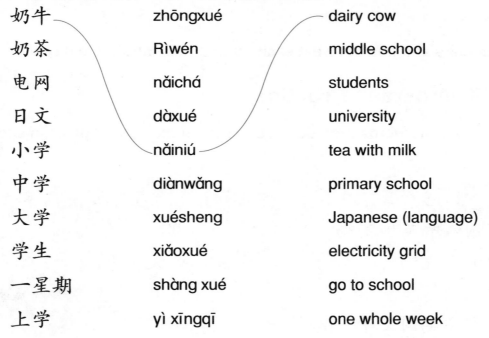

奶牛	zhōngxué	dairy cow
奶茶	Rìwén	middle school
电网	nǎichá	students
日文	dàxué	university
小学	nǎiniú	tea with milk
中学	diànwǎng	primary school
大学	xuésheng	Japanese (language)
学生	xiǎoxué	electricity grid
一星期	shàng xué	go to school
上学	yì xīngqī	one whole week

翻译练习 Translation

Say the following sentences in Chinese and then write them out in characters.

1. What is your major? Mine is English literature.
2. What do you do on Saturdays?
3. Do you drink tea or milk?
4. Miss Wang writes Chinese characters every evening.
5. I don't drink Chinese tea in the morning.
6. Do you read books or watch TV in the evenings?

汉字知识 Chinese Characters

会意字（一） Ideative Characters (1)

Ideatives are also called associative compounds because as the name suggests, they are usually made up of two or more independent characters. The meaning of an ideative is normally derived from the meanings of its constituent characters.

There are two types of ideative characters. The first type of ideative consists of two or more of the same characters being combined to express the idea of multiplicity or quantity, as illustrated below:

Character 1	+	Character 2	=	Ideative
人 *rén* people		人 *rén* people		从 *cóng* follow
人 *rén* people		从 *cóng* follow		众 *zhòng* masses

If 木 is a pictograph for a tree, guess what the other two Chinese characters below mean?

木 *mù* tree　　　　林 *lín* ____　　　　森 *sēn* ____

写字练习 Character Writing Exercise

Can you recognise these characters? Test yourself to see if you are able to write the Pinyin and English meanings above each character. Afterwards, copy each character, following its stroke order. Try to gain a feel for the structure of each character when copying it, especially those consisting of two or three components.

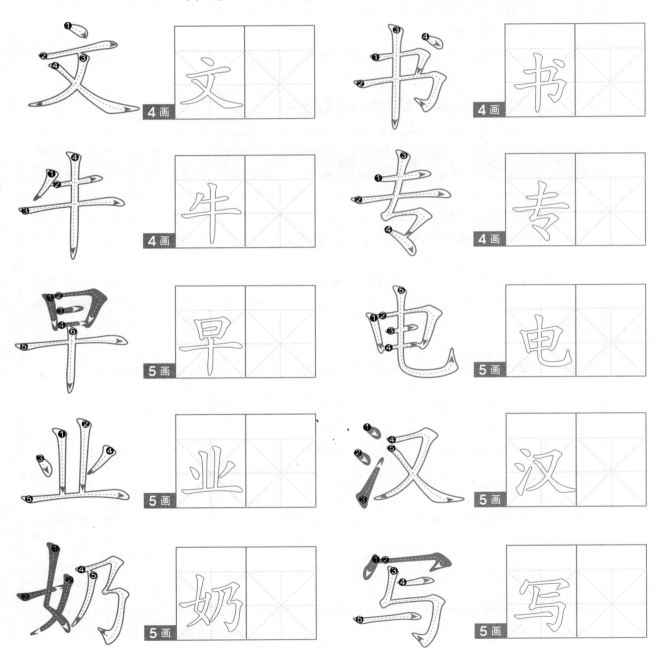

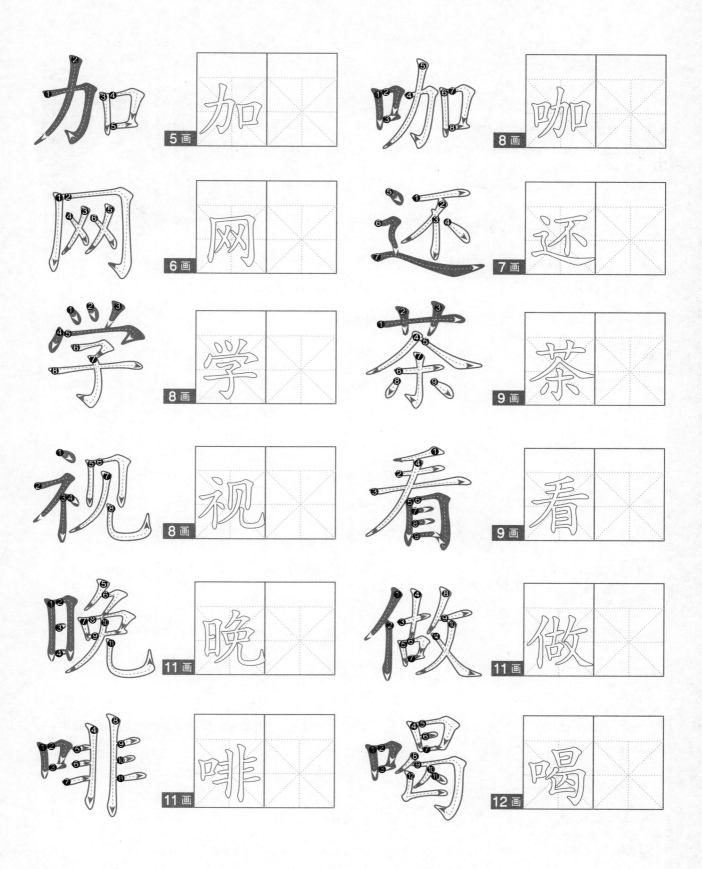

06

第六课   我会说一点儿汉语

Learning objectives

To talk about what one likes or dislikes doing
To talk about what one can do or should do
To talk about one's favourite sports

生词 New Words

会	huì	*m.v/n*	can, may; meeting	
想	xiǎng	*m.v/v*	would like to, intend; think; miss	
要	yào	*m.v/v*	want	
应该	yīnggāi	*m.v*	should	应 should 该 should
喜欢	xǐhuan	*v*	like	喜* like 欢* huān happy
认识	rènshi	*v*	know	认 recognise 识 shí know
说	shuō	*v*	speak	
打	dǎ	*v*	play (games); hit	
踢	tī	*v*	kick; play (football)	
汉语	Hànyǔ	*n*	Chinese (language) 语 language	
外语	wàiyǔ	*n*	foreign language 外 outside; foreign	
日语	Rìyǔ	*n*	Japanese (language)	
法语	Fǎyǔ	*n*	French 法 France; law; method	
足球	zúqiú	*n*	football 足 foot 球 ball	
网球	wǎngqiú	n	tennis	
一点儿	yì diǎnr	*n/adj*	a bit; a bit of 点 point; hour 儿 non-syllabic suffix	
可是	kěshì	*conj*	but 可 may, can	
为什么	wèishénme	*q.w*	why 为 for, on account of	
一起	yìqǐ	*adv*	together	
因为	yīnwèi	*conj*	because 因 cause, reason for	

句型 Speech Patterns

S	Adv	MV	V	O
我 Wǒ		会 huì	说 shuō	汉语。 Hànyǔ .
她 Tā	不 bù	想 xiǎng	打 dǎ	网球。 wǎngqiú 。
他们 Tāmen	都 dōu	要 yào	学 xué	中文。 Zhōngwén .

Modal verbs are used here in the same way as in English. That is, the modal verb goes before the action verb and the adverb precedes the modal verb if used.

S	MV	不	MV	V	O
你 Nǐ	会 huì	不 bu	会 huì	说 shuō	汉语? Hànyǔ ?
他 Tā	想 xiǎng	不 bu	想 xiǎng	打 dǎ	网球? wǎngqiú ?
我们 Wǒmen	应 yīng	不 bu	应该 yīnggāi	学 xué	汉语? Hànyǔ ?

When there is a modal verb in an affirmative-negative choice question, it is the modal verb that takes the affirmative-negative form rather than the action verb. When the modal verb is a two-character word, you can repeat just the first character.

S	喜欢	V	O
我 Wǒ	喜欢 xǐhuan	踢 tī	足球。 zúqiú 。
我 Wǒ	喜欢 xǐhuan	看 ká	电视。 diànshì 。
他 Tā	喜欢 xǐhuan		我。 wǒ .

While you can say 喜欢 + an object, you normally have to say 喜欢 + a verb and an object in Chinese when an action is implied. Therefore, you should say 喜欢喝茶 rather than 喜欢茶 to avoid ambiguity.

S	TW	Adv	V	好吗
我们 Wǒmen	今天 jīntiān		看电视, kàn diànshì ,	好吗? hǎo ma ?
我们 Wǒmen		一起 yìqǐ	写汉字, xiě hànzì ,	好吗? hǎo ma ?
我们 Wǒmen		一起 yìqǐ	上网, shàng wǎng ,	好吗? hǎo ma ?

好吗 is used at the end of a statement to make a suggestion, similar to "shall we?" in English.

补充词汇 Additional Vocabulary

Sports (with action verb 打)			Sports (with other action verbs)		
dǎ páiqiú	打排球	play volleyball	huá bīng	滑冰	skate
dǎ pīngpāngqiú	打乒乓球	play table tennis	huá shuǐ	滑水	surf
dǎ yǔmáoqiú	打羽毛球	play badminton	huá xuě	滑雪	ski
dǎ gǎnlǎnqiú	打橄榄球	play rugby	pǎo bù	跑步	jog
dǎ lánqiú	打篮球	play basketball	yóu yǒng	游泳	swim

对话 1 Dialogue One

李：王京，你是英国人，为什么要①学汉语？

王：我喜欢学外语。我会说法语，也会说一点儿日语。

李：你会说日语？你认识②汉字吗？

王：不认识。

李：我会说一点儿③汉语，可是我也不认识汉字。

王：你想学汉字吗？

李：我的老师说我应该学，可是我不想学。

王：为什么？

李：我喜欢汉字，可是汉字不喜欢我。

对话 2 Dialogue Two

王：小李，你喜不喜欢踢足球？

李：不喜欢，我不会踢。

王：你喜欢打网球吗？

李：我喜欢看，不喜欢打。

王：为什么？

李：因为我不太会打④。

王：我也不太会，我们一起学，好吗？

李：好。

语法注释 Grammar Notes

① 想 **and** 要 —Both of the words are modal verbs. 想 means "would like to", while 要 means "want". 想 is more polite than 要 in its usage.

② 认识 —认识 and 知道 are often translated as "know" in English, but they are quite different in Chinese. 知道 means "having a knowledge of something" while 认识 is used for recognising or identifying people, characters and roads.

For example:

我不认识他。
I don't know him. (personally)
我知道他是英国人。
I know he is English.

③ 一点儿 —Some Chinese words have an additional character 儿 added to them, especially in spoken language. However 儿 doesn't form an independent syllable. It is usually pronounced as an "r" ending to the syllable in front of it.

In some cases, it distinguishes the meaning of words.

For example:

这(zhè) **means "this"** 这儿(zhèr) **means "here"**
那(nà) **means "that"** 那儿(nàr) **means "there"**

In spoken English, the 一 in 一点儿 is usually omitted. Thus it is common to hear 我会说点儿法语 or 你想喝点儿什么？

④ 我不太会打(网球) —I don't play (tennis) very well. When 太 is used in a negative sentence, it is similar to 很, but less strong in emphasis.

⑤ **Additional tone changes** — 一 is pronounced with a first tone on its own, but it becomes a fourth tone when it precedes a first tone, a second tone or a third tone syllable (e.g., *yì zhī, yì pán, yì běn*). Like 不, 一 becomes a second tone when it precedes a fourth tone syllable (e.g., *yí gè*).

文化知识 Cultural Note

"天"字的魅力 The Fascinating Character 天

天 is an ideographic character that reflects the way the ancient Chinese viewed the relationship between human beings and the sky (Heaven) above. The character implies "The highest", and it means both "sky" and "gods". 天 is formed by a horizontal line on top of the character 大 which shows a person with arms fully outstretched horizontally. Therefore 天 is a world above human beings and is thus holy and mysterious.

练习 Exercises

口语练习 Speaking Practice

Work in pairs or small groups, using modal verbs to talk about the following topics:

1. What you can do or cannot do (speak a foreign language, cook and etc.);

2. What you like to do and dislike doing;

3. Please ask and answer the following questions in Chinese:

A	B
What is your name?	Are you from Beijing?
Where are you from?	Do you drink milk in the mornings?
When is your birthday?	Is tomorrow your birthday?
What do you drink in the mornings?	Are you going to play tennis tonight?
What is your major (study)?	Is your major Chinese literature?
What are you going to do tomorrow?	Do you know our English teacher or not?
Shall we play tennis together tonight?	Do you play tennis or football?
Would you like to watch TV tonight?	Do you watch TV every evening?
Do you like to read or surf the Internet?	Are you going to read or write tonight?
I can speak Chinese, what about you?	Can't you speak English?

听力练习 Listening Practice

1. Listen and repeat. Pay attention to the tone of 不 in the last line.

1) a. bù shuō   b. bù hē   c. bù tī
2) a. bù xué   b. bù lái   c. bù yóuyǒng
3) a. bù hǎo   b. bù dǎ   c. bù xǐhuan
4) a. bú shì   b. bú kàn   c. bú rènshi

2. Listen to the short statements or dialogues and then mark each of the following sentences as true (T) or false (F).

1. Xiao Li should know how to write Chinese characters.   (   )

2. She likes to play tennis, but she does not like to play football.　　(　　)

3. Teacher Wang doesn't know Japanese at all.　　　　　　　　　　(　　)

4. He can recognise Chinese characters, but can't write them.　　　(　　)

5. He drinks Chinese tea every morning.　　　　　　　　　　　　(　　)

6. He is going to watch TV this evening.　　　　　　　　　　　　(　　)

语法练习 Grammar Practice

1. Match the verbs on the list with the nouns below (verbs may be used more than once).

Verb list:　学　看　打　喝　写　说　踢　上

1) ＿＿＿＿汉语　　　2) ＿＿＿＿足球　　　3) ＿＿＿＿网球

4) ＿＿＿＿电视　　　5) ＿＿＿＿汉字　　　6) ＿＿＿＿网

7) ＿＿＿＿中国茶　　8) ＿＿＿＿咖啡　　　9) ＿＿＿＿法语

10) ＿＿＿＿牛奶　　　11) ＿＿＿＿书　　　12) ＿＿＿＿老师

2. Complete the following dialogues by filling in blanks with the appropriate words from the list.

Word list:　喜欢　可是　一点儿　踢　打　会

1)　我会说＿＿＿＿英语。

2)　我们今天＿＿＿＿网球，好吗?

3)　她会说汉语，＿＿＿＿她不认识汉字。

4)　你想学＿＿＿＿足球吗?

5)　我＿＿＿＿上网，可是我太太不喜欢上网。

6)　我们都＿＿＿＿说英语。

认读练习 Matching Exercise

Please follow the example and link each of the Chinese words with their corresponding Pinyin and meanings in English.

英语	Yīngyǔ	there
地球	Fǎguó	English
法国	nǎr	viewpoint
法人	fǎrén	study of law
法学	nàr	the Earth
看法	shī-shēng	teachers & students
师生	zhèr	France
那儿	dìqiú	where
哪儿	fǎxué	legal person
这儿	kànfa	here

翻译练习 Translation

Say the following sentences in Chinese and then write them out in characters.

1. My Chinese teacher doesn't like to play football.
2. She can't speak French, but she can speak Japanese.
3. I'd like to learn Chinese characters.
4. Doctor Li can speak a little Chinese.
5. He surfs the Internet every evening.
6. I would like to have some Chinese tea.

阅读 Reading

你晚上都做什么？

　　你们好！我的中文名字叫李大明。我是法国人，今年十九岁，是伦敦大学的学生。我的专业是汉语，我也学中国文学。我会说法语、英语、汉语和一点儿日语。我喜欢学外语，也很喜欢打球。我星期一晚上打篮球，星期二晚上看法文书，星期三晚上打网球，星期四晚上学中文，星期五晚上踢足球，星期六晚上上网看中国电影(diànyǐn—film)，星期天晚上我写汉字。你晚上都做什么？

Please answer the following questions based on the information in the text above.

1. Who is Li Daming and where is he from?
2. How old is he and what is his major?
3. What languages can he speak?
4. What does he do on Thursday and Friday evenings?
5. What do you do in the evenings?

汉字知识 Chinese Characters

会意字（二） Ideative Characters (2)

The second type of ideative usually consists of two different characters used together to express an idea that "combines" the meanings of the constituent characters. For example:

Character 1 +			Character 2			= Ideative		
人	rén	person	木	mù	tree	休	xiū	rest
小	xiǎo	small	土	tǔ	soil	尘	chén	dust
手	shǒu	hand	目	mù	eye	看	kàn	look

Some ideative characters are culturally defined, as illustrated below:

Character 1		+	Character 2		=	Ideative		
田	tián	field	力	lì	strength	男	nán	man
女	nǚ	woman	子	zǐ	child	好	hǎo	good
人	rén	people	言	yán	speech	信	xìn	trust

写字练习 Character Writing Exercise

Can you recognise these characters? Test yourself to see if you are able to write the Pinyin and English meanings above each character. Afterwards, copy each character, following its stroke order. Try to gain a feel for the structure of each character when copying it, especially those consisting of two or three components.

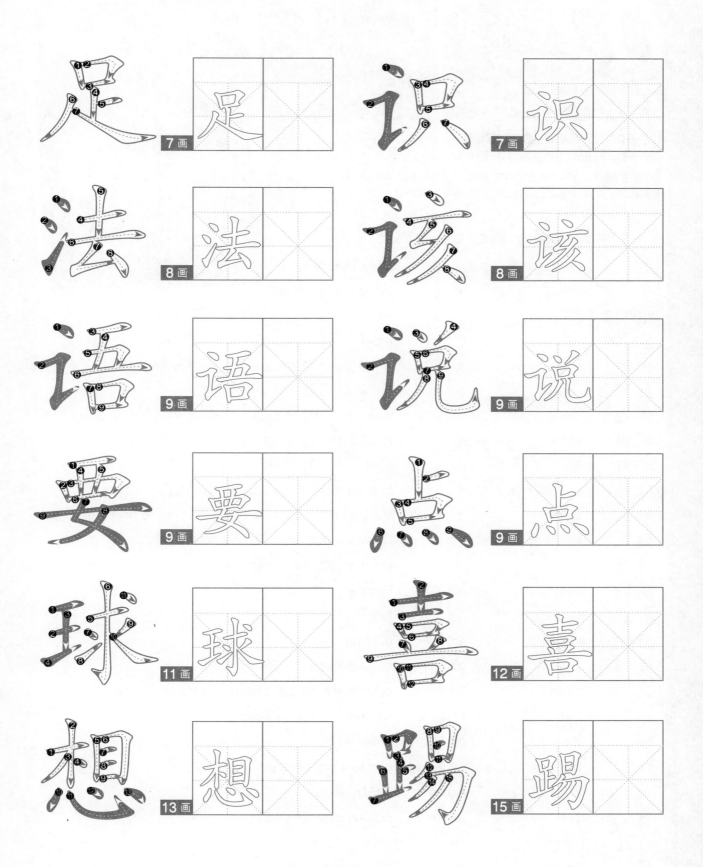

07

第七课　你们有北京烤鸭吗?

Learning objectives

To order simple food and drinks in a restaurant
To talk about your likes and dislikes for certain foods
To learn to use the Chinese measure words

生词 New Words

有	yǒu	v	have; there be
了	le	pt	forms a complement
吃	chī	v	eat
点	diǎn	v	order
白酒	báijiǔ	n	white spirits 白 white　　酒 alcoholic drink
红酒	hóngjiǔ	n	red wine　　红 red
啤酒	píjiǔ	n	beer　　啤* beer　　五星啤酒 Five Stars Beer
烤鸭	kǎoyā	n	roast duck 烤 roast; bake　　鸭 duck
牛肉	niúròu	n	beef　　肉 meat
红烧肉	hóngshāoròu	n	braised meat in soy sauce 烧 to cook; to braise
炒饭	chǎofàn	n	stir-fried rice 炒 to stir fry 饭 cooked rice; food; meal
白菜	báicài	n	Chinese cabbage 菜 vegetable; dish; food
青菜	qīngcài	n	green vegetable 青 green
法国	Fǎguó	p.n	France
有名	yǒumíng	adj	famous
好吃	hǎochī	adj	delicious
没	méi	adv	negation word for 有
只	zhǐ/zhī	adv/m.w	only; m.w for birds, cats and some other animals
个	gè	m.w	a general measure word
瓶	píng	m.w/n	bottle of; bottle
杯	bēi	m.w/n	glass of, cup of; cup
碗	wǎn	m.w/n	bowl of; bowl
盘	pán	m.w/n	dish of, plate of; plate
这儿	zhèr	l.w	here
还	hái	adv	still, also, as well

句型 Speech Patterns

S	有	O
他们 Tāmen	有 yǒu	烤鸭。 kǎoyā.
他们 Tāmen	有 yǒu	中文书。 Zhōngwén shū.
她 Tā	有 yǒu	电视。 diànshì.

有 means "to have", but it also means "there exists" as you will see in the next lesson.

S	没	(有)	O
他们 Tāmen	没 méi	(有) yǒu	姐姐。 jiějie.
你 Nǐ	没 méi	(有) yǒu	中国茶。 Zhōngguó chá.
我们 Wǒmen	没 méi	(有) yǒu	啤酒。 píjiǔ.

The negative form of 有 is 没有, and it is common to omit 有 in negative sentences in spoken Chinese.

S	有没有	O
你们 Nǐmen	有没有 yǒu méi yǒu	中国菜? Zhōngguó cài?
你们 Nǐmen	有没有 yǒu méi yǒu	弟弟? dìdi?
他们 Tāmen	有没有 yǒu méi yǒu	啤酒? píjiǔ?

This is a simple alternative question structure for the verb 有, to be followed by a noun.

S	V	Num	MW	O
我 Wǒ	要 yào	(一) yì	杯 bēi	啤酒。 píjiǔ.
我们 Wǒmen	要 yào	三 sān	碗 wǎn	米饭。 mǐfàn.
我 Wǒ	要 yào	(一) yì	只 zhī	烤鸭。 kǎoyā.

In Chinese, most nouns cannot be modified by a number directly, and a measure word is needed between the noun and the number. While the number can be omitted if it is "one", the measure word can't.

补充词汇 Additional Vocabulary

hóng pútaojiǔ	红葡萄酒	red wine		sānmíngzhì	三明治	sandwich
bái pútaojiǔ	白葡萄酒	white wine		dàngāo	蛋糕	cake
júzizhī	橘子汁	orange juice		dànchǎofàn	蛋炒饭	egg fried rice
píngguǒzhī	苹果汁	apple juice		chǎomiàn	炒面	stir-fried noodles
hóngchá	红茶	black tea		jiǎozi	饺子	Chinese dumpling
lǜchá	绿茶	green tea		shuǐguǒ	水果	fruit

对话 1 Dialogue One

Waiter：你们好！你们想喝点儿什么②？

李：有没有中国白酒？

W：对不起，我们只有中国红酒。

谢：我们今天就喝中国红酒吧。

W：你们要几瓶？

王：我们只有四个人，先要一瓶吧③。

W：好，你们想吃点儿什么？

方：你们有北京烤鸭吗？

W：有。我们这儿的北京烤鸭很有名。

李：你们这儿还有什么很有名？

W：我们的红烧肉也很有名，很好吃④。

谢：好，我们要一个红烧肉、一只烤鸭。

王：再点一个炒青菜、一个牛肉炒白菜、四碗炒饭。

对话 2 Dialogue Two

W：先生，您想吃点儿什么？

李：我要一盘牛肉炒饭。

W：好。您想喝点儿什么？

李：有啤酒吗？

W：有。英国啤酒、中国啤酒，我们都有。

李：有没有中国五星啤酒？

W：有。

李：太好了⑤！我要一杯五星啤酒。

语法注释 Grammar Notes

① **Measure word** —Measure words also exist in English, but are usually used for uncountable nouns such as water and tea. For example a <u>cup</u> of tea, a <u>bottle</u> of water, and a <u>flock</u> of sheep. While measure words are required for most nouns in Chinese, the commonly used ones are only about 40, many of which are nouns themselves. In addition, they also follow certain general guidelines. This means that the use of measure words is not as complicated as they may seem to be.

② 你们想喝点儿什么？ —What would you like to drink? This is a polite way to ask the question. You can ask in a direct way 你们要喝点儿什么？ which means "what do you want to drink?"

③ 先要一瓶吧 —先 is an adverb here meaning first. It can be used together with 再 to indicate the sequence of two actions.

> **For example:**
> 我们先喝酒，再吃饭。

④ 好吃 **and** 好喝 — The meaning of each word is very obvious, referring to "good to eat" and "good to drink". This construction (adj + verb) is common in Chinese, and the compound is usually used as an adjective, or stative verb as is called in some other books.

⑤ 太好了！ — It / This is wonderful! This is an expression without subject. 太 here means very, super. You can substitute 好 with other adjectives.

> **For example:**
> 太大了！ Too big!
> 太好吃了！ Very delicious!
> 太多了！ Too many/much!

文化知识 - Cultural Note

中国人的饮食   Food in Chinese Life

Food remains an important aspect of Chinese life. If you take a look around any city in China, you will see many restaurants. For years, food was a concern for the state as well as for ordinary people. As a result of this, eating is still a major event during many traditional Chinese celebrations, such as the New Year, weddings, birthday parties, and even get-togethers with friends. In fact, food is so pervasive that asking someone if she or he has eaten is still a casual greeting one often hears amongst the Chinese people.

练习 Exercises

 ### 口语练习 Speaking Practice

1. Working in pairs, talk about what kind of drinks and food you like.

2. Here is a menu. Working in a small group, pretend that you are at a Chinese restaurant with one of you acting as a waiter or waitress. Practise ordering food.

菜 单
(Càidān-MENU)

中国红酒	158元/瓶	法国红酒	56元/杯
英国红酒	198元/瓶	五星啤酒	10元/瓶
中国白酒	96元/瓶	可乐	10元/瓶
烤鸭	158元/只	炒牛肉	36元/盘
炒青菜	18元/盘	红烧肉	35元/盘
牛肉炒饭	18元/盘	炒饭	12元/盘

听力练习 Listening Practice

1. Listen and repeat, paying attention to the tones of 一.

1) 一杯中国茶	2) 一只烤鸭
3) 一盘青菜	4) 一瓶啤酒
5) 我会说一点儿中文	6) 我们一起学汉字
7) 一个中国人	8) 一个英国人

2. Listen to the short dialogues and then choose the correct answer for each question.

1)	a. roast duck	b. white wine	c. stir-fried rice
2)	a. British beer	b. Chinese red wine	c. Chinese beer
3)	a. stir-fried beef	b. braised meat in sauce	c. roast duck
4)	a. beer	b. English tea	c. Chinese tea
5)	a. Japanese book	b. Chinese book	c. English book
6)	a. her birthday	b. his birthday	c. They like roast duck

语法练习 Grammar Practice

1. Choose the correct word from a, b or c to complete each of the following sentences.

1) 我们要三＿＿炒饭。	a.杯	b.瓶	c.盘
2) 他们都＿＿会说英语。	a.不	b.喜欢	c.没
3) 我要一＿＿啤酒。	a.杯	b.只	c.盘
4) 我＿＿一只烤鸭。	a.想	b.喜欢	c.要
5) 王小明＿＿有弟弟。	a.不	b.没	c.都
6) 英国酒好喝，可是英国菜不太＿＿。	a.好喝	b.好吃	c.喜欢

2. Use 没 and 不 to change the following sentences into their negative forms.

1) 今天我们有烤鸭。

2) 我要日本啤酒。

3) 你喜欢踢足球吗？

4) 他们有中国茶。

5) 他天天看电视。

6) 我们今天晚上写汉字。

认读练习 Matching Exercise

Please follow the example and link each of the Chinese words with their corresponding Pinyin and meanings in English.

早饭	zǎofàn	wine glass
晚饭	hǎokàn	good-looking
茶杯	chábēi	breakfast
酒杯	yāròu	supper
酒瓶	fànwǎn	duck meat
酒会	jiǔpíng	tea cup
饭碗	jiǔbā	wine bottle
酒吧	wǎnfàn	pub
鸭肉	jiǔbēi	rice bowl/job
好看	jiǔhuì	cocktail party

翻译练习 Translation

Say the following sentences in Chinese and then write them out in characters.

1. Do you have Chinese beer? I would like to have a glass of it.
2. We don't have stir-fried beef with green vegetables today.
3. Tomorrow is my birthday. Shall we eat Chinese food?
4. I like to drink Chinese beer and eat Beijing roast duck.
5. We would like to have four bottles of French red wine.
6. I like French food very much, as it is very delicious.

阅读 Reading

我喜欢吃中国饭

你们好！你们认识我，我是李大明。我很喜欢吃中国饭、喝中国茶。我天天喝中国茶，可是我很少(hěn shǎo—seldom)吃中国饭，因为我不会做。我很想学，可是没有老师。我的中文老师也不会做，她说她家(jiā—family)她先生做饭，她只会吃，不会做。上个星期六(last Saturday)我们老师家有一个晚会(party)。晚会上(at the party)有很多好吃的饭菜。中国菜有北京烤鸭、红烧牛肉、炒饭，还(in addition)有炒青菜。英国菜有烤牛肉和三明治。有的人(some people)吃英国饭，有的人吃中国饭，有的人英国饭、中国饭都吃，可是我只吃中国饭，你们应该知道为什么。

Please answer the following questions based on the information in the above text.

1. What does Li Daming like to eat and drink?
2. Why does he seldom have Chinese food?
3. Is Daming's Chinese teacher a good cook?
4. What kinds of food were there at the party?
5. Who only ate Chinese food at the party and why?

汉字知识 Chinese Characters

形声字 Semantic-phonetic Compounds

A semantic-phonetic compound is also referred to as a pictophonetic compound. It usually consists of a semantic radical (which could be a pictograph) and a phonetic element. Characters constructed in this way represent well over half of the frequently used Chinese characters (different statistics claim from 60% to about 90%).

Semantic radicals can be independent characters or symbols. Semantic radicals indicate a semantic field, or what they are associated with. The phonetic element, —sometimes an independent character on its own, provides some clue as to the pronunciation of the compound.

Sementic radical	Phonetic component	Semantic-phonetic compound	Meaning	Pinyin
氵—water	曷 hé	渴	thirsty	kě
口—mouth	曷 hé	喝	drink	hē
火—fire	少 shǎo	炒	stir-fry	chǎo

写字练习 Character Writing Exercise

Can you recognise these characters? Test yourself to see if you are able to write the Pinyin and English meanings above each character. Afterwards, copy each character, following its stroke order. Try to gain a feel for the structure of each character when copying it, especially those consisting of two or three components.

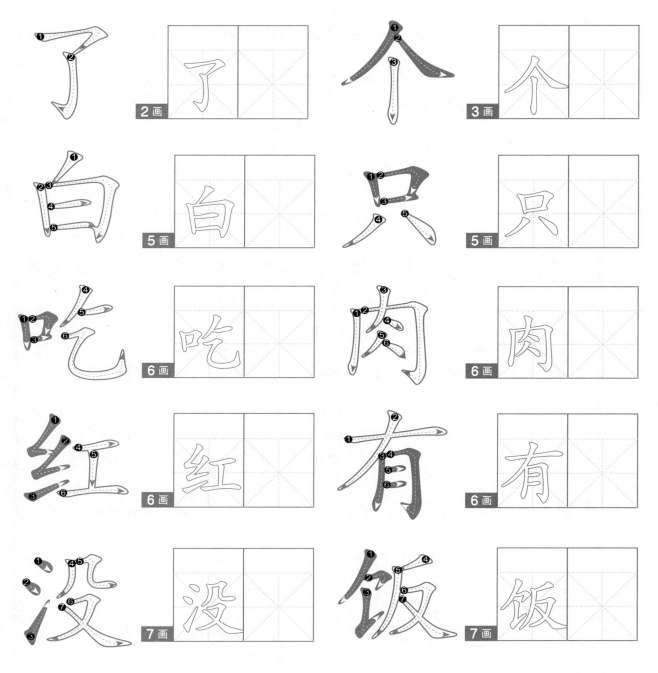

08

第八课　我家有四口人

Learning objectives

To talk about your family
To say if you are tired or thirsty
To offer someone something to eat or drink

生词 New Words

累	lèi	*adj*	tired	
忙	máng	*adj*	busy	
渴	kě	*adj*	thirsty	
饿	è	*adj*	hungry	
爸爸	bàba	*n*	dad	爸 dad
妈妈	māma	*n*	mum	妈 mum
家	jiā	*n/m.w.*	home; family; house; specialist in a field	
男朋友	nán péngyou	*n*	boyfriend	男 man, male 朋*/友*yǒu / 朋友 friend
女朋友	nǚ péngyou	*n*	girlfriend	女 woman, female
哥哥	gēge	*n*	elder brother	哥 elder brother
作家	zuòjiā	*n*	writer	作 to do; to make; to write
工作	gōngzuò	*n*	work	工 work; labour
商人	shāngrén	*n*	businessman	商 business; commercial
律师	lǜshī	*n*	lawyer	律 law; rule
可爱	kě'ài	*adj*	lovely	爱 to love
狗	gǒu	*n*	dog	
猫	māo	*n*	cat	
条	tiáo	*m.w*	for various long narrow things	
口	kǒu	*m.w/n*	for family members; mouth	
有点儿	yǒudiǎnr	*adv*	somewhat; a bit	
两	liǎng	*num*	two (used in front of a measure word)	

句型 Speech Patterns

S	Adv	Adv	Adj
医生 Yīshēng		很 hěn	累。 lèi .
我 Wǒ		有点儿 yǒudiǎnr	渴。 kě .
我们 Wǒmen	都 dōu	很 hěn	饿。 è .

Unlike in English, most Chinese adjectives can be used as predicates to indicate states (also termed as stative verbs). However, such adjectives are normally modified by an adverb of degree, unless it is followed by a sentence of contrast, for example: 你饿，我不饿。

S	Adj	吗
你 Nǐ	饿 è	吗？ ma ?
你们 Nǐmen	渴 kě	吗？ ma ?
李小姐 Lǐ xiǎojiě	饿 è	吗？ ma ?

The question form of an S+Adj speech pattern is created by adding 吗 to the end of the sentence, as in other speech patterns.

S	TW	Adv	Adv	Adj
我 Wǒ			不 bú	饿。 è .
我 Wǒ	今天 jīntiān		不 bù	忙。 máng .
他们 Tāmen		都 dōu	不 bù	渴。 kě .

The negative form of an S+Adj speech pattern is formed by adding 不 before the adjective (verb). This is different from the negative form of an S+N speech pattern where 是 should be used.

S	Adj	不	Adj
你们 Nǐmen	忙 máng	不 bu	忙？ máng ?
他的中文 Tā de Zhōngwén	好 hǎo	不 bu	好？ hǎo ?
北京烤鸭 Běijīng kǎoyā	贵 guì	不 bu	贵？ guì ?

不 should be used to form an affirmative-negative question.

补充词汇 Additional Vocabulary

wàijiāoguān	外交官	diplomat		piányi	便宜	cheap
mìshū	秘书	secretary		gāoxìng	高兴	glad
zhíyuán	职员	office worker		shūfu	舒服	comfortable
hùshi	护士	nurse		piàoliang	漂亮	beautiful
jǐngchá	警察	police		nánkàn	难看	ugly, bad looking
sījī	司机	driver		nánchī	难吃	taste bad (food)

对话 1 Dialogue One

李：小王，你家有几口人？

王：我家有四口人①，爸爸、妈妈、哥哥和我。

李：你哥哥也是学生吗？

王：不，他是医生。我爸爸、妈妈也是医生。

李：你哥哥的女朋友也是医生吧？

王：他还没有女朋友呢②。你爸爸妈妈做什么工作？

李：我爸爸是商人，我妈妈是作家。

王：你们家只有三口人吗？

李：不，我还有一个姐姐，她是律师。

王：我家还有一条可爱的小狗，你家有没有狗？

李：我家没有狗，我妈不喜欢狗，她喜欢猫。我家有两只猫③。

对话 2 Dialogue Two

李：小王，你今天忙不忙？

王：忙，我今天很忙。你呢？

李：我不太忙。你累不累？

王：我不累，可是我有点儿④渴。

李：喝点儿茶吧，我这儿有茶⑤。

王：我不爱喝茶。你有咖啡吗？

李：有，你饿不饿？我这儿还有吃的⑥。

王：我不饿，谢谢。

李：不客气。

语法注释 Grammar Notes

① **我家有四口人** —有 here means "there are" as mentioned in the previous lesson.

For example:
北京有很多外国人.
There are a lot of foreigners in Beijing.

② **他还没有女朋友呢** —还没有……呢 means "not ... yet". It is used to indicate that the assumption made by the other speaker is not right at the moment, though the situation may change in the future.

③ **两只猫** —When the number "two" is used together with a measure word, 两 is normally used instead of 二.

For example:
两杯茶、两瓶酒、两个人

④ **有点儿/一点儿** —有点儿 means "somewhat" or "a little bit", and it is used as an adverbial phrase to modify adjectives, while 一点儿, which means "a bit" is used to modify nouns.

For example:
我有点儿饿, 我想吃 (一) 点儿饭。

⑤ **我这儿有茶** —这儿 means "here", and it is a location word. Thus, it precedes the relevant verb.

⑥ **吃的** —The element after 的 is usually understood in context. In this case it refers to food, and therefore it can be omitted. This construction of verb + 的 acts as a noun, and it is a very common construction in spoken Chinese.

For example:
我很渴, 你有没有喝的?

文化知识 Cultural Note

中国的家庭 Chinese Families

Due to the implementation of the family planning policy in the mid-1970s, the average size of families in China's mainland has become much smaller than extended traditional families were. Having one child per couple is very common in urban areas, but in rural areas, especially economically underdeveloped areas, a couple may have two or three children. Generally speaking however, the decrease in the number of people in Chinese families has been notable. As a result of this, many of the kinship terms depicting the complicated relationships in families are rarely used nowadays.

练习 Exercises

口语练习 Speaking Practice

1. Working in pairs, introduce the following details of a few members of your family or your friends to each other.

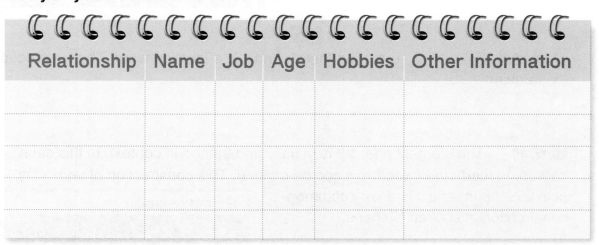

Relationship	Name	Job	Age	Hobbies	Other Information

2. Share with the class what you have learnt from your partner in the first exercise.

听力练习 Listening Practice

1. Listen and repeat, paying attention to the tone of the first syllable in each word.

烤鸭 kǎoyā	很多 hěn duō	老师 lǎoshī	网球 wǎngqiú
打球 dǎ qiú	想学 xiǎng xué	很好 hěn hǎo	想你 xiǎng nǐ
法语 Fǎyǔ	炒饭 chǎofàn	炒菜 chǎocài	几岁 jǐ suì
晚上 wǎnshang	姐姐 jiějie	喜欢 xǐhuan	

2. Listen to the short dialogues and then choose the correct answer for each question.

1) a. 六口　　　　　 b. 五口　　　　　 c. 四口
2) a. 老师　　　　　 b. 作家　　　　　 c. 医生
3) a. 渴　　　　　　 b. 忙　　　　　　 c. 饿
4) a. 弟弟　　　　　 b. 妹妹　　　　　 c. 哥哥
5) a. 一只　　　　　 b. 三只　　　　　 c. 没有
6) a. 中医医生　　　 b. 中学老师　　　 c. 中学生

语法练习 Grammar Practice

1. Choose the correct word from a, b or c to complete each of the following sentences.

1) 我_____累。
　　a. 一点儿　　　 b. 没　　　　　　 c. 不

2) 他有_____妹妹。
　　a. 两个　　　　 b. 二个　　　　　 c. 二口

3) 他们_____饿。
　　a. 一点儿　　　 b. 有点儿　　　　 c. 有

4) 我女朋友有一_____猫。
　　a. 条　　　　　 b. 只　　　　　　 c. 口

5) 你爸爸_____什么工作?
　　a. 是　　　　　 b. 做　　　　　　 c. 应该

6) 我有姐姐_____妹妹,可是我没有哥哥。
　　a. 都　　　　　 b. 也　　　　　　 c. 和

2. Fill in each blank with an appropriate word to complete the sentences.

1) 他姐姐_____中学老师。

2) 医生今天不_____忙。

3) 我很累，_____很渴。

4) 小李的哥哥_____有女朋友。

5) 你_____什么工作?

6) 李明的妈妈有两条_____。

 认读练习 **Matching Exercise**

Please follow the example and link each of the Chinese words with their corresponding Pinyin and meanings in English.

说法 ———	shuōfǎ	idea
想法	àirén	male student
做法	zuòyè	way of saying
国家	zuòfa	good friend
好友	xiǎngfǎ	way of doing something
爱人	guójiā	female student
男生	gōngrén	state, country
女生	hǎoyǒu	homework
作业	nánshēng	worker
工人	nǚshēng	spouse

翻译练习 **Translation**

Say the following sentences in Chinese and then write them out in characters.

1. What do your parents do?

2. Mrs Wang has two cats and three dogs.

3. I'm a bit busy today.

4. There are five people in his family.

5. I'm neither hungry nor thirsty.

6. Li Xiaoying is 24 years old. She has two elder sisters, one younger brother, and three younger sisters.

阅读 Reading

我家有几口人？

我叫方明英，今年二十岁。我家有爸爸、妈妈、姐姐、妹妹和我。我爸爸是英国人，我妈妈是中国人，他们都是大学老师。我爸爸是英文老师，我妈妈是中文老师。我姐姐是律师，她的男朋友是作家，他是俄罗斯（Éluósī—Russia）人，他会说英语、法语和一点儿汉语，他很喜欢学外语。我妹妹今年八岁，是个小学生。我们家还有一条狗和两只猫。我妹妹说："我们家应该是九口人。"你说我们家有几口人？

Please answer the following questions based on the information in the above text.

1. What do Fang Mingying's parents do?
2. How many brothers and sisters does she have?
3. Where is her elder sister's boyfriend from?
4. Do they have any pets at home?
5. What is your answer to the question at the end of the passage?

 汉字知识 **Chinese Characters**

偏旁部首 Radicals

The Chinese word for radical is 偏旁部首(piānpáng bùshǒu). Radicals play a very important role in compound characters, so being able to recognise radicals helps in the learning and understanding of new characters, especially when looking up new characters in dictionaries. There are traditionally 214 radicals, but between 40 to 50 are the most frequently used.

偏旁 refers to the side radicals, which can be either semantic or phonetic in nature, and are usually found on the left or the right side of compound characters. The following table lists four common side semantic radicals together with the compounds in which they occur.

Semantic radical	Meaning	Examples		
火	fire	炒	烧	烤
氵	water	渴	酒	汉
女	woman	姐	妈	妹
口	mouth	吧	吃	喝

写字练习 Character Writing Exercise

Can you recognise these characters? Test yourself to see if you are able to write the Pinyin and English meanings above each character. Afterwards, copy each character, following its stroke order. Try to gain a feel for the structure of each character when copying it, especially those consisting of two or three components.

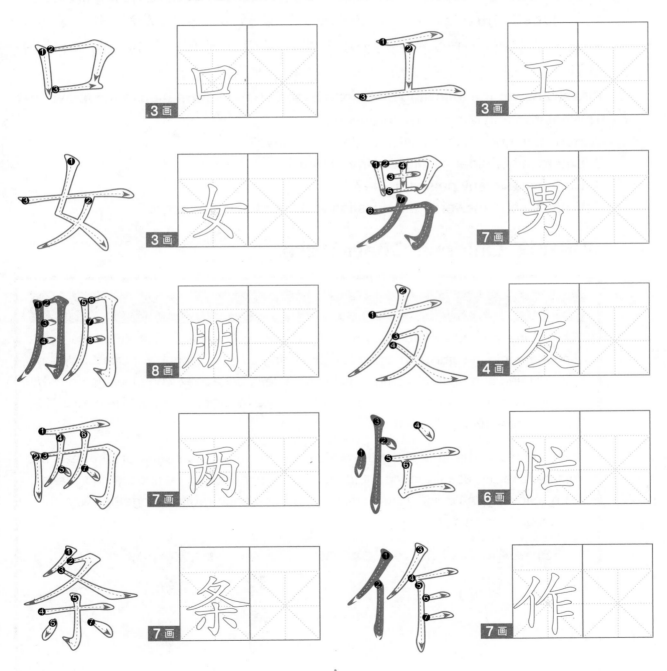

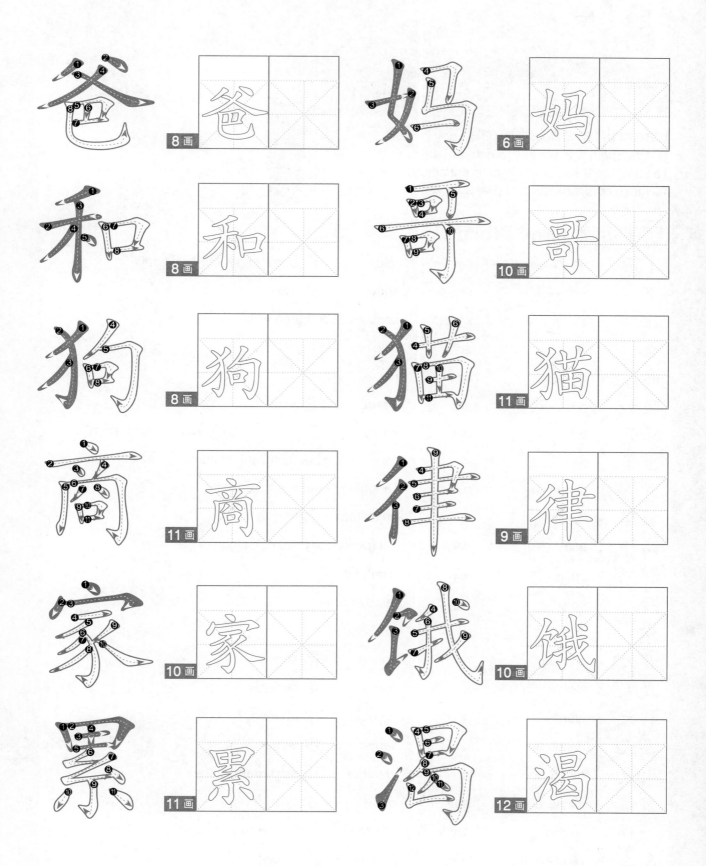

09

第九课　北京夏天比伦敦热

Learning objectives

To talk about the weather in different seasons
To compare the weather in different places
To make comparisons and give suggestions

生词 New Words

下雨	xià yǔ	*v-o*	rain	下 to fall; to get off　雨 rain
下雪	xià xuě	*v-o*	snow	雪 snow
比	bǐ	*v/prep*	compare; compared with	
冷	lěng	*adj*	cold	
热	rè	*adj*	hot	
暖和	nuǎnhuo	*adj*	warm	暖 warm
漂亮	piàoliang	*adj*	pretty	漂* smart　亮 liàng bright, shiny
个子	gèzi	*n*	(of a human being) height; stature　子 a noun suffix
青青	Qīngqing	*p.n*	Qingqing (a name)	
篮球	lánqiú	*n*	basketball　篮 basket	
高	gāo	*adj*	tall (person or building), high	
胖	pàng	*adj*	stout; fat	
瘦	shòu	*adj*	thin (a person)	
少	shǎo	*adj*	few; little	
春天	chūntiān	*n*	spring	春 spring
夏天	xiàtiān	*n*	summer	夏 summer
秋天	qiūtiān	*n*	autumn	秋 autumn
冬天	dōngtiān	*n*	winter	冬 winter
天气	tiānqì	*n*	weather	气 air; breath
常常	chángcháng	*adv*	often	常 often
一样	yíyàng	*adj/adv*	the same	样* (m.w/n) type; manner
怎么样	zěnmeyàng	*q.w*	How is it?	怎* how; why

🔊 句型 Speech Patterns

A	比	B	Adv	Adj
中国 Zhōngguó	比 bǐ	英国 Yīngguó		大 dà 。
北京夏天 Běijīng xiàtiān	比 bǐ	伦敦(夏天) Lúndūn (xiàtiān)	还 hái	热 rè 。
他 Tā	比 bǐ	我 wǒ	还 hái	高 gāo 。

Chinese comparisons follow the simple pattern of "A 比 B + Adj", as shown on the left. 还 can be used before the adjective, but not after the adjective, to indicate the sense of "even more".

A	比	B	Adj	Comp
北京 Běijīng	比 bǐ	伦敦 Lúndūn	热 rè	多了 duō le 。
他弟弟 Tā dìdi	比 bǐ	他 tā	瘦 shòu	一点儿 yìdiǎnr 。
我哥哥 Wǒ gēge	比 bǐ	我 wǒ	大 dà	一岁 yí suì 。

Unlike in English, Chinese adverbial modifiers of degree (such as "much" and "a bit") appear as complements after the adjectives modified.

A	没(有)	B	Adj
我哥哥 Wǒ gēge	没(有) méi (yǒu)	我 wǒ	高 gāo 。
伦敦夏天 Lúndūn xiàtiān	没(有) méi (yǒu)	北京(夏天) Běijīng (xiàtiān)	热 rè 。
英国 Yīngguó	没(有) méi (yǒu)	法国 Fǎguó	大 dà 。

Negative comparison is typically expressed with 没有. In spoken Chinese, 有 is often omitted.

A	和	B	一样	Adj
她 Tā	和 hé	我 wǒ	一样 yíyàng	大 dà 。
他哥哥 Tā gēge	和 hé	他 tā	一样 yíyàng	高 gāo 。
北京夏天 Běijīng xiàtiān	和 hé	上海 Shànghǎi	一样 yíyàng	热 rè 。

The pattern on the left is used to express the idea that the two items compared are the same, in some respect.

🔊 补充词汇 Additional Vocabulary

liángkuai	凉快	cool	ǎi	矮	short (height)
mēnrè	闷热	muggy, close	fù/yǒu qián	富/有钱	rich
gānzào	干燥	dry	qióng/méi qián	穷/没钱	poor
cháoshī	潮湿	damp, humid	yǒuyòng	有用	useful
qīng	轻	light (weight)	yuǎn	远	far
zhòng	重	heavy (weight)	jìn	近	near, close

对话 1 Dialogue One

方：小王，那是谁？是你女朋友吗？

王：是的^①。她叫青青，很喜欢打篮球。

方：真漂亮！她个子很高，

王：她和我一样高，我有点儿胖。

方：你不胖，你比我瘦多了。

王：你有没有女朋友？

方：有，我女朋友是王京的妹妹。

王：是吗？她比你小多了吧？

方：不多，她只比我小三岁。

对话 2 Dialogue Two

李：小王，北京的天气怎么样？

王：夏天很热，冬天很冷。

李：北京夏天比伦敦热吗^②？

王：比伦敦热多了^③！

李：上海呢？

王：上海比北京还热。

李：北京的春天怎么样？

王：春天很好，很暖和。
可是没有伦敦暖和^④。

李：常常下雨吗？

王：春天雨很少，可是夏天雨很多。

李：北京冬天下不下雨？

王：冬天不下雨，冬天下雪。

李：我喜欢下雪天。
北京的秋天怎么样？

王：秋天很好，不冷不热。

语法注释　Grammar Notes

① 是的—This is a common expression of confirmation, similar to 对. 的 is a particle here expressing assurance and confirmation.

② 北京夏天比伦敦(夏天)热吗—夏天 can be omitted after 伦敦 as it is clear from the context. 北京夏天很热 means pretty much the same thing as 北京的夏天很热, but their sentence structures are different. There will be more detailed discussion on this point later.

③ (北京)夏天比伦敦热多了—了 is a particle used in a number of ways in Chinese. Here it goes together with the word 多 to indicate the degree of the adjective.

④ (北京的春天)没有伦敦暖和—The negative form for a comparative sentence with 比 is "A 没有 B + Adj", as shown above. However, there is an "A 不比 B + Adj" sentence structure which is used to indicate that A and B are not very different. This structure is only used to respond to what is perceived as incorrect.

Compare:

1) 我没有小李高。I am not as tall as Xiao Li.
2) A: 你太太比你高。　A: Your wife is taller than you.
   B: 她不比我高。　　B: She is not taller than I am.
   (They might be of the same height.)

文化知识　Cultural Note

中文里的"胖"字　The Chinese Word 胖

Traditionally, this word has been used as a compliment to suggest that someone looks very healthy and is not short of food. In a country where there are many mouths to feed, it has always been a blessing if one can afford to put on some weight. As times have changed however, the Chinese concept of health and well-being has changed, too. Nowadays, while the word is still very much used by some people, particularly parents, in a commendatory way, others, such as the younger generation and especially young women have become very sensitive to the word, often taking it as a derogatory term, just as people do in the West.

练习 Exercises

口语练习 Speaking Practice

1. Working in pairs, talk about the weather in London or other places you know.

2. Work in small groups to describe someone or something (food, drink, etc.) by means of comparison. For example:

I am tall.

I am taller than my elder brother.

I am a bit taller than my elder brother.

I am much taller than my elder brother.

I am not as tall as my elder brother.

听力练习 Listening Practice

1. Listen and repeat, paying attention to the tones of the first syllable in each word.

1)	先生 xiānsheng	医生 yīshēng	他们 tāmen	商人 shāngrén
2)	什么 shénme	名字 míngzi	学生 xuésheng	朋友 péngyou
3)	怎么 zěnme	我们 wǒmen	暖和 nuǎnhuo	姐姐 jiějie
4)	谢谢 xièxie	认识 rènshi	漂亮 piàoliang	太太 tàitai

2. Listen to the short dialogues and then choose the correct answer for each question.

1)	a. 我高	b. 我弟弟高	c. 我们一样高
2)	a. 北京冷	b. 伦敦冷	c. 北京暖和
3)	a. 她姐姐高	b. 她高	c. 她们一样高
4)	a. 冬天	b. 春天	c. 夏天
5)	a. 下雨天	b. 热天	c. 下雪天
6)	a. 法国	b. 英国	c. 北京

语法练习 Grammar Practice

1. Choose the correct word from a, b or c to complete each of the following sentences.

1) 她的狗比我的狗_____漂亮。

    a. 没有   b. 比   c. 还

2) 我女朋友_____我高一点儿。

    a. 没有   b. 比   c. 和

3) 我弟弟_____我爸爸胖。

    a. 没有   b. 也   c. 一样

4) 北京夏天比伦敦热_____了。

    a. 不多   b. 多   c. 很多

5) 伦敦的秋天和北京的秋天_____好，不冷不热。

    a. 一点儿   b. 多   c. 一样

6) 我哥哥比我姐姐_____。

    a. 大两岁   b. 两岁大   c. 一样大

2. Use the given information to make up sentences using comparisons.

	A	B	Adj
1)	夏天	春天	热
2)	中国	法国	大
3)	北京冬天	伦敦冬天	冷
4)	伦敦春天	伦敦冬天	漂亮
5)	中国菜	英国菜	好吃
6)	我	我哥哥	小

认读练习 Matching Exercise

Please follow the example and link each of the Chinese words with their corresponding Pinyin and meanings in English.

大小 ——	dàxiǎo	heating
大家	xiǎoshuō	queen (head of state)
生气	nuǎnqì	size
暖气	nǚwáng	calligraphy
春雨	jiāshū	stingy
女王	xiǎoqì	letter (from/to) home
小气	shēngqi	angry
小说	chūnyǔ	spring rain
书法	dàjiā	novel
家书	shūfǎ	all of us

翻译练习 Translation

Say the following sentences in Chinese and then write them out in characters.

1. China is larger than Britain.
2. I like spring very much. It is neither cold nor hot.
3. I am as tall as my boyfriend.
4. He is very tall. His brother is even taller than him.
5. Roast duck is more expensive than stir-fried beef with green vegetables.
6. What is the weather like in London in winter? London is much warmer than Beijing in winter.

阅读 Reading

我姐姐和北京的天气

　　我姐姐叫李小英，她是律师，她在（zài—in）北京工作。她说她很喜欢北京的冬天。北京的冬天很冷，常常下雪。伦敦的冬天比北京暖和，可是常常下雨，我和我姐姐都不喜欢下雨天，我们喜欢下雪天。北京的夏天很热，比伦敦热多了。我姐姐有点儿胖，她不喜欢太热的天气，所以 (suǒyǐ—so) 她不太喜欢北京的夏天。北京的春天和秋天很好，不冷不热，也不常常下雨。我姐姐说，春天的北京很漂亮，我想明年春天去 (qù—go) 北京看我姐姐，也看看 (have a look) 漂亮的北京。

Please answer the following questions based on the information in the above text.

1. Where is Li Xiaoying working and what kind of work is she doing?
2. What is the weather like in Beijing in winter?
3. Why doesn't Li Xiaoying like Beijing's summer?
4. How is the weather in London compared to Beijing in the summer?
5. What is the narrator going to do next spring and why?

 ## 汉字知识 Chinese Characters

声旁 Phonetic Components

Though there is no hard and fast rule in Chinese as to how a sound is determined, many independent characters can provide clues to the pronunciation of the semantic-phonetic compounds they help to form. They usually retain finals (vowels), which seem to be consistent, while initials may change depending on which semantic radicals they are combined with. One example is given in the table below.

Semantic Radical		Phonetic Component	Compound	Pinyin	Meaning
rain	雨		雹	báo	hail
food	饣		饱	bǎo	full (not hungry)
hand	扌	包 bāo (bag)	抱	bào	take in one's arms
mouth	口		咆	páo	shout, roar
foot	足		跑	pǎo	run
water	氵		泡	pào	soak, marinate

写字练习 Character Writing Exercise

Can you recognise these characters? Test yourself to see if you are able to write the Pinyin and English meanings above each character. Afterwards, copy each character, following its stroke order. Try to gain a feel for the structure of each character when copying it, especially those consisting of two or three components.

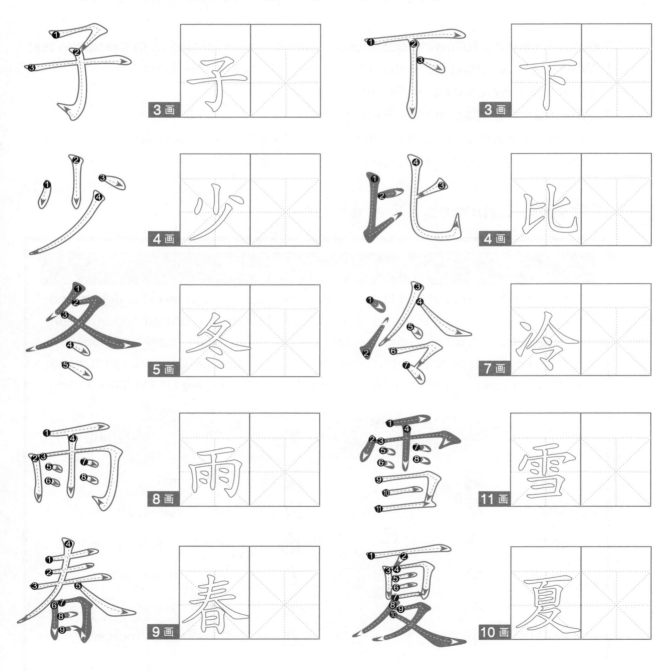

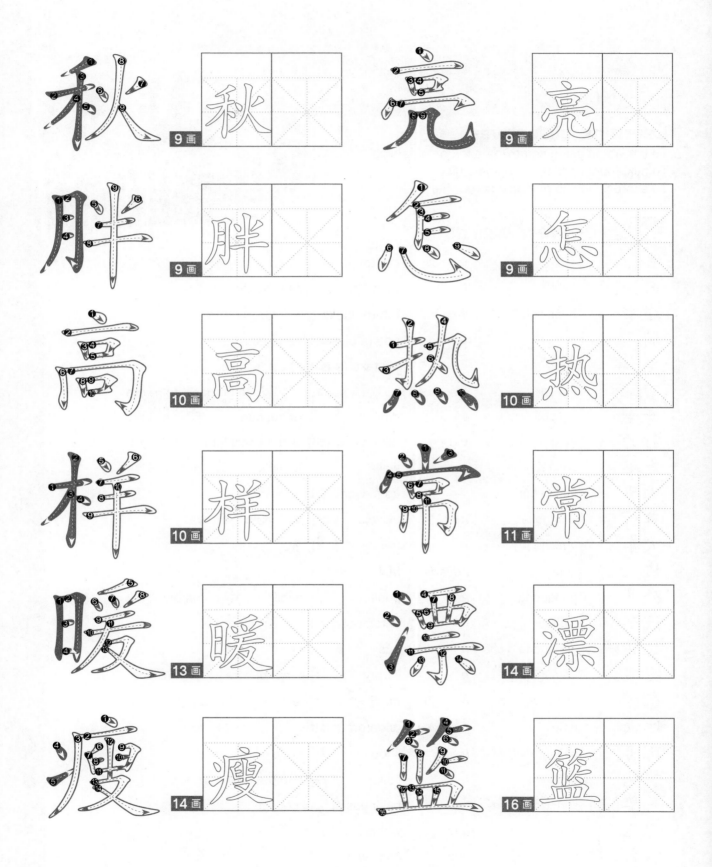

秋 9画
胖 9画
高 10画
样 10画
暖 13画
瘦 14画

亮 9画
怎 9画
热 10画
常 11画
漂 14画
篮 16画

10

第十课　你怎么去商店？

Learning objectives

To talk about going somewhere to do something
To talk about coming to do something
To express how to go/come somewhere

生词 New Words

去	qù	v	go (to)
来	lái	v	come (the opposite direction of 去)
还书	huán shū	v-o	return books　　还 to return
骑	qí	v	ride (a bicycle, horse etc.)
坐	zuò	v	sit; take (bus etc.)
回家	huí jiā	v-o	go back home　　回 to go back, to return
开车	kāi chē	v-o	drive　　开 drive; open　　车 vehicle
打的	dǎ dí	v-o	take a taxi (的 is the short form of 的士 taxi)
走路	zǒu lù	v-o	walk　　走 to walk　　路 road
上班	shàng bān	v-o	go to work　　班 shift; class
自行车	zìxíngchē	n	bicycle　　自 self, auto　　行 walk
火车	huǒchē	n	train　　火 fire
快	kuài	adj/adv	fast
公共	gōnggòng	adj	public　　公 public　　共 common
汽车	qìchē	n	automobile, car　　汽 steam
公共汽车	gōnggòng qìchē	n	bus
图书馆	túshūguǎn	n	library　　图 map; picture　　馆 building
东方	Dōngfāng	n	the East, the Orient　　东 east
地铁	dìtiě	n	underground train　　铁 iron
商店	shāngdiàn	n	shop　　店 shop
学院	xuéyuàn	n	college　　院 compound; courtyard
商学院	shāngxuéyuàn	n	business school/college
哪儿	nǎr	q.w	where
怎么	zěnme	q.w	how; why

句型 Speech Patterns

S	Adv	来/去	QW/Place
你 Nǐ		去 qù	哪儿? nǎr?
我 Wǒ	不 bú	去 qù	商店。 shāngdiàn.
他们 Tāmen	明天 míngtiān	去 qù	商学院。 shāngxuéyuàn.

Please note the position of the question word when asking about a place, and the way in which the answer is given.

TW	S	来/去	Place
明年 Míngnián	我们 wǒmen	去 qù	中国。 Zhōngguó.
明天 Míngtiān	你 nǐ	去 qù	什么地方? shénme dìfang?
今晚 Jīnwǎn	她 tā	来 lái	我家。 wǒ jiā.

Please note a time word can go before the subject for the purpose of emphasising time, but other adverbs can not.

S	TW	来/去	Place	V	O
我 Wǒ	明天 míngtiān	去 qù	图书馆 túshūguǎn	还 huán	书。 shū.
他 Tā	明年 míngnián	去 qù	北京 Běijīng	学 xué	汉语。 Hànyǔ.
她 Tā	天天 tiāntiān	来 lái	我家 wǒ jiā	看 kàn	我。 wǒ.

The pattern (to go somewhere to do something) is nearly the same as in English except for the position of the time word.

S	TW	V	O	来/去	Place
我 Wǒ	天天 tiāntiān	坐 zuò	地铁 dì tiě	去 qù	学院。 xuéyuàn.
我 Wǒ	明天 míngtiān	骑 qí	车 chē	去 qù	商店。 shāngdiàn.
他 Tā	今晚 jīnwǎn	开 kāi	车 chē	来 lái	伦敦。 Lúndūn.

You have to put the means of transport before 去 as you will require this before you arrive at your destination. If you put the means of transportation after 去, then it becomes the purpose of going somewhere.

补充词汇 Additional Vocabulary

zuò chē	坐车	by vehicle	xiàwǔ	下午	afternoon
zuò chūzūchē	坐出租车	by taxi	kāi huì	开会	have/attend a meeting
zuò fēijī	坐飞机	by plane	jiè shū	借书	borrow books
zuò chuán	坐船	by boat/ship	mǎi dōngxi	买东西	shopping
shàngwǔ	上午	morning	chū chāi	出差	go on a business trip
zhōngwǔ	中午	noon	dù jià	度假	go on a holiday

对话 1 Dialogue One

王：小李，你去哪儿？

李：我去商店。

王：你去哪家商店？

李：我去那家东方商店。你去哪儿？

王：我去图书馆。

李：今天星期六，你去图书馆做什么？

王：我去图书馆还书。

李：你怎么去？我有自行车，你骑我的车去吧。

王：谢谢，我喜欢走路，我还是走路去吧①。

对话 2 Dialogue Two

李：老王，你回家吗？

王：不，我先去商学院再回家②。

李：你去商学院做什么？

王：我去看一个朋友。他是那儿的老师。

李：明天没有地铁，你怎么来上班？

王：我坐火车来。你呢？

李：我想坐公共汽车来。

王：你怎么不打的来③？
打的比坐公共汽车快多了。

李：可是也贵多了。

王：对。你不是有汽车吗④？
为什么不开车来？

李：因为我还不会开车。

语法注释 Grammar Notes

① 我还是走路去吧—还是……吧 is a construction, meaning "it would be better if...". It is used for a choice made after consideration. It can also be used to make a suggestion, meaning "you had better..." .

For example:

1) 我们还是先吃饭吧。
2) 你还是坐汽车去吧。

② 我先去商学院再回家—再 is used here before the verb to refer to a deferred action, or to mean "then" rather than "again" as in 再见.

For example:

1) 今天很冷，我明天再去。
2) 我们先去北京，再去东京。

③ 你怎么不打的来？ —Here 怎么 means why, not how. When 怎么 is used in this sense, it indicates a sense of surprise. 为什么 also means why, but it does not usually imply this sense of surprise.

Compare the following sentences:

1) 你怎么去法国？
Why are you going to France?
2) 你怎么想去法国？
Why would you think of going to France?
3) 你为什么想去法国？
Why are you thinking of going to France?

④ 你不是有汽车吗？ —不是……吗？ is a construction used for confirmation or emphasis, sometimes with a sense of surprise or dissatisfaction.

For example:

1) 你不是中国人吗？
Are you not Chinese?
2) 你不是有书吗？
Don't you already have the book?

文化知识 Cultural Note

中国的出租车 The Chinese Taxi

The formal term for taxis in Chinese is 出租车 (chūzūchē). While it is correct to say 我天天坐出租车去上班 (I go to work by taxi every day), many Chinese nowadays would use the more colloquial term 打的, which is an expression taken from Cantonese. So, for the same sentence above, you are more likely to hear Chinese people say 我天天打的去上班. In fact there are many expressions in contemporary Chinese that have been taken from other languages or dialects, which illustrates how Chinese interacts with other languages.

练习 Exercises

口语练习 Speaking Practice

Working in pairs, talk about your weekly schedule. The following is an example.

A: 星期一你去哪儿?

B: 星期一我先去医院看朋友,再去大学。

A: 你怎么去?   B: 坐地铁去。

Time	Transport	Place 1	Purpose	Place 2
星期一	地铁	医院	看朋友	大学
星期二				
星期三				
星期四				
星期五				
星期六				
星期天				

听力练习 Listening Practice

1. Listen and repeat, paying attention to the "r" ending.

1)   nǎr   你去哪儿?

2)   zhèr   这儿东西贵不贵?

3)   yìdiǎnr   我会说一点儿中文。

4)   yǒudiǎnr   今天有点儿冷?

5)   fànguǎnr   我不喜欢那家饭馆儿。

2. Listen to the short dialogues and then choose the correct answer for each question.

1)   a. 图书馆   b. 商店   c. 商学院

2)   a. 坐地铁   b. 骑车   c. 开车

3) a.还书　　　　b.看电视　　　　c.看朋友

4) a.图书馆　　　b.商学院　　　　c.回家

5) a.不喜欢骑车　　b.没有自行车　　c.不会骑车

6) a.坐公共汽车快　b.坐火车贵　　　c.没有火车

语法练习 Grammar Practice

1. Choose the correct word from a, b or c to complete each of the following sentences.

1) 她们_____地铁去商店。

 a.骑　　　b.坐　　　c.有

2) 我明天上午去图书馆_____。

 a.还书　　b.喝茶　　c.吃饭

3) 你今天骑车_____家吗?

 a.去　　　b.上　　　c.回

4) 我们_____路去上班吧。

 a.走　　　b.坐　　　c.骑

5) 你们_____去北京?

 a.什么　　b.来　　　c.怎么

6) 我男朋友星期三_____这儿看我。

 a.去　　　b.来　　　c.走

2. Use appropriate question words to ask questions about the underlined parts of the following sentences.

1) <u>他</u>明天开车去商学院看朋友。

2) 他<u>明天</u>开车去商学院看朋友。

3) 他明天<u>开车</u>去商学院看朋友。

4) 他明天开车去<u>商学院</u>看朋友。

5) 他明天开车去商学院看<u>朋友</u>。

6) 他明天开车去商学院看<u>朋友</u>。

认读练习 Matching Exercise

Please follow the example and link each of the Chinese words with their corresponding Pinyin and meanings in English.

地图	shūdiàn	tram, trolley
书店	fǎxuéyuàn	pedestrian
行人	wàiyǔ xuéyuàn	hospital
回国	fàndiàn	map
电车	yīyuàn	restaurant, hotel
医院	xíngrén	medical school
医学院	huí guó	bookshop
饭店	dìtú	law school
法学院	diànchē	go back to one's country
外语学院	yīxuéyuàn	school of foreign languages

翻译练习 Translation

Say the following sentences in Chinese and then write them out in characters.

1. I shall not drive to school tomorrow.
2. Where are you going? I am going to the library to return books.
3. Mr Li will take the tube home today.
4. He goes to the library to read every day.
5. My mother can't ride a bike, so she goes to work by bus every day.
6. Wang Ming won't come to work tomorrow. He is going to Beijing this evening.

阅读 Reading

我喜欢骑车去上班

很多人喜欢开车去上班，可是我喜欢骑车去。春夏秋冬，我差不多 (chàbuduō—nearly) 天天都骑自行车去上班。伦敦没有地铁吗？有！伦敦的公共汽车不多吗？很多！可是我就是不喜欢坐。伦敦坐地铁的人很多，夏天坐地铁很热，<u>再说</u>（besides），坐地铁也很贵。我也不喜欢坐伦敦的公共汽车，伦敦路上的行人（pedestrians）和汽车太多，骑车常常比坐公共汽车<u>还快</u>（even faster）。今天是星期六，我不上班。我要骑车去我女朋友家看她爸爸妈妈，晚上我们一起去看电影。

Please answer the following questions based on the information in the above text.
1. According to the text, how does the narrator go to work every day?
2. Why doesn't the narrator like the underground?
3. What does the narrator think about the buses?
4. What does he plan to do today?
5. How do you go to work and what is your plan for this Saturday?

汉字知识 Chinese Characters

简繁体汉字
Simplified and Complicated Forms of Chinese Characters

There are two forms of Chinese characters in use, simplified characters (简体字—jiǎntǐzì) and complicated characters (繁体字—fántǐzì). The simplified characters became official in the mid-1950s in the PRC, and are now widely accepted and used abroad.

Compared with complicated characters, simplified characters generally have a reduced number of strokes. The simplification of some 2,000 characters was based upon a number of principles in line with the characteristics of Chinese characters and the actual use of those characters in daily life. The table below lists some characters in both forms and records their number of strokes.

Simplified characters	学	医	后	尘	书
No. of strokes	8	7	6	6	4
English	study	medical	behind	dust	book
Pinyin	xué	yī	hòu	chén	shū
Complicated characters	學	醫	後	塵	書
No. of strokes	16	18	9	14	10

写字练习 Character Writing Exercise

Can you recognise these characters? Test yourself to see if you are able to write the Pinyin and English meanings above each character. Afterwards, copy each character, following its stroke order. Try to gain a feel for the structure of each character when copying it, especially those consisting of two or three components.

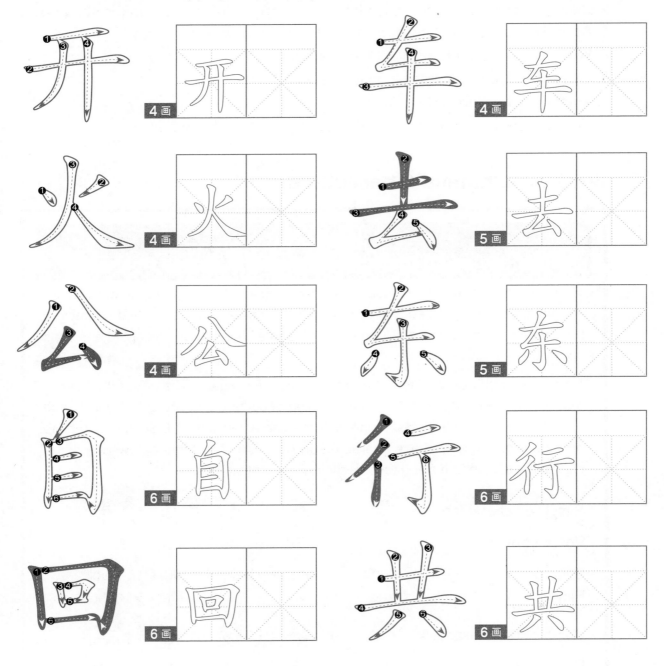

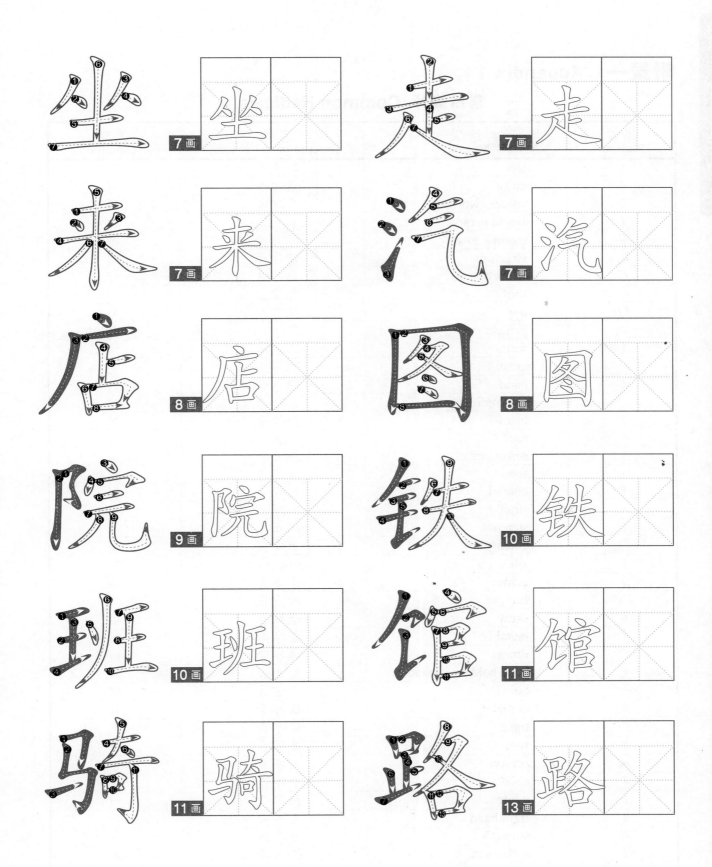

附录一 Appendix 1

常用偏旁 Common Radicals

部首 Radical	语义 Meaning	名称 Description in Chinese	例字 Example
冫	ice	两点水	冰
刂	knife	立刀旁	到
讠	speech, word	言字旁	语
亻	single person	单立人	你
阝	mound, town	耳刀旁	都
廴	structure	建字旁	建
厂	factory	偏厂儿	厅
冖	roof	秃宝盖	写
勹	bag	包字头	句
厶	private	私字儿	么
氵	water	三点水	法
艹	grass	草字头	英
扌	hand	提手旁	打
辶	walk quickly	走之旁	这
忄	heart	竖心旁	忙
宀	roof	宝盖头	客
彡	ornament	斜三撇	须
饣	food	食字旁	饭
犭	animal	反犬旁	猫
尚	small	小字头	光
彳	step out	双立人	很
囗	enclosure	大口框	国
纟	silk	绞丝旁	纪
牜	cattle	牛字旁	牲
灬	fire	四点底	热
礻	show	示补旁	被
钅	metal	金字旁	铁
疒	illness	病字旁	瘦
攵	hand holding a stick	反文旁	敦
穴	hole	穴宝盖	空
衤	clothing	衣补旁	补
虍	tiger	虎字头	虎
𧾷	foot	足字旁	踢
𠆢	person	人字头	今
孑	child	子字旁	孩
白	white	白字旁	的
又	right hand	又字旁	对
力	strength	力字底	男
土	soil, earth	提土旁	地
弓	bow	弓字旁	张

部首 Radical	语义 Meaning	名称 Description in Chinese	例字 Example
广	wide, vast	广字旁	庆
口	mouth	口字旁	吗
夕	sunset	夕字旁	名
门	door	门字框	闲
工	work	工字旁	功
女	woman	女字旁	好
巾	cloth, towel	巾字旁	帽
尸	corpse	尸字头	屋
山	mountain	山字旁	峨
马	horse	马字旁	骑
王	king; jade	王字旁	环
日	sun	日字旁	明
月	moon; flesh	月字旁	期
气	air	气字头	氛
心	heart	心字底	您
户	single door	户字头	房
车	vehicle	车字旁	辆
父	father	父字头	爸
贝	seashell	贝字底	贵
方	square	方字旁	放
火	fire	火字旁	烤
木	wood, tree	木字旁	林
石	stone, rock	石字旁	碗
目	eye	目字底	看
田	field	田字头	累
皿	container, utensil	皿字底	盘
禾	cereal	禾木旁	利
鸟	bird	鸟字旁	鸭
立	stand	立字旁	站
耳	ear	耳字旁	聪
虫	insect	虫字旁	蛤
竹	bamboo	竹字头	篮
舟	boat	舟字旁	船
米	rice	米字旁	籽
身	body	身字旁	射
雨	rain	雨字头	雪
鱼	fish	鱼字旁	鲜
革	leather	革字旁	鞋
酉	container	酉字旁	醒

附录二 Appendix 2

组词游戏 Word Game

How many Chinese words and phrases can you find in the following table? They can only be formed with neighbouring characters, however characters can be used more than once, and the formation can be in any direction, up down, left right, and diagonally.

视	踢	的	打	人	铁	地	方	东	北
没	电	足	篮	吧	下	汽	火	红	京
店	书	看	球	网	上	班	车	烧	烤
友	朋	女	王	做	晚	早	吃	肉	鸭
好	男	国	律	炒	饭	白	喝	牛	奶
医	中	学	法	师	生	菜	酒	啤	茶
中	生	文	语	老	人	红	青	杯	碗
先	日	字	汉	小	天	有	字	回	大
岁	月	亮	姐	天	气	名	专	家	会
年	漂	妹	期	今	明	业	作	开	没
饭	五	星	去	年	好	商	店	公	有
馆	多	球	回	很	累	人	雪	共	打
书	少	来	冷	贵	春	雨	下	汽	开
图	猫	狗	热	姓	骑	自	行	车	坐

附录三　Appendix 3

听力原文　Listening Scripts

Lesson One

听力练习　Listening Practice

1. Listen to the recording and then choose the phrase you have heard in each group.

1) 你好　　　　　　　　　2) 谢谢

3) 您好　　　　　　　　　4) 再见

5) 不客气　　　　　　　　6) 我很好

Lesson Two

听力练习　Listening Practice

Listen to the short dialogues and then mark each of the following sentences as true (T) or false (F).

1. 女：您贵姓?　　　　　　　　男：我姓李。

2. 男：你叫什么名字?　　　　　女：我叫王英。

3. 男：他叫什么名字?　　　　　女：他叫方国伦。

4. 女：他姓什么?　　　　　　　男：他姓布什。

5. 女：我叫王英。你叫什么?　　男：我叫李贵。

6. 女：我姓张, 你呢?　　　　　男：我也姓张。

Lesson Three

听力练习　Listening Practice

Listen to the short dialogues and then mark each of the following sentences as true (T) or false (F).

1. 男：小姐, 你叫什么名字?　　女：我叫方小英。

2. 男：谢老师是哪国人?　　　　女：她是法国人。

3. 男：王先生是什么地方人?　　女：他是北京人。

4. 男：王太太是医生吗?　　　　女：不是, 她是老师。

5. 男：方小姐是不是英国人?　　女：她是英国人。

6. 男：他们都是中国人吗?　　　女：不, 他们都不是中国人。

Lesson Four

听力练习　Listening Practice

Listen to the short dialogues and then choose the correct answer for each question.

1. 女：今天几号？　　　　　　　男：今天十月一号。

   男：What is the date today?

2. 女：王英的生日是哪天？　　　男：二月十七日。

   男：When is Wang Ying's birthday?

3. 女：明天是星期二吗？　　　　男：不是，明天是星期三。

   男：What day is tomorrow?

4. 女：她是谁？　　　　　　　　男：她是王老师，王老师是北京人。

   男：Where is Teacher Wang from?

5. 女：李英，星期六是几号？　　男：星期六是六月二十九号。

   男：What is the date this Saturday?

6. 女：今天是谁的生日？　　　　男：今天是我弟弟的生日。

   男：Whose birthday is it today?

Lesson Five

听力练习　Listening Practice

Listen to the short dialogues and then mark each of the following sentences as true (T) or false (F).

1. 男：你学中文吗？　　　　　　女：不，我不学中文。
2. 男：你今天晚上看不看电视？　女：我不看电视，我看书。
3. 男：李英学什么专业？　　　　女：她学英国文学。
4. 男：王京天天晚上都学中文吗？女：不，他星期天晚上不学。
5. 男：你早上喝什么？　　　　　女：我喝牛奶。
6. 男：你晚上写不写汉字？　　　女：不写，我早上写。

Lesson Six

听力练习　Listening Practice

2. Listen to the short statements or dialogues and then mark each of the following sentences as true (T) or false (F).

1) 小李是中国人，他应该会写汉字。
2) 她喜欢打网球，可是她不喜欢踢足球。
3) 王老师会说汉语、英语，也会说一点儿日语。
4) 女：你认识汉字吗？　　　　　男：我认识汉字，可是我不会写汉字。
5) 女：你喜欢喝什么？　　　　　男：中国茶，我天天早上都喝中国茶。
6) 女：我们晚上一起看电视，好吗？男：我今天晚上想看书，不想看电视。

Lesson Seven

听力练习　Listening Practice

2. Listen to the short dialogues and then choose the correct answer for each question.

1) 女：先生，您想吃点儿什么？　　　男：我要一盘炒饭。

　　男：What did the man want?

2) 男：小姐，有中国啤酒吗？　　　女：对不起，没有，我们只有英国啤酒。

　　男：What did the restaurant have?

3) 女：先生，你们这儿什么菜很有名？　男：我们这儿的红烧肉很有名。

　　男：What is their famous dish?

4) 女：小王，你喜不喜欢喝中国茶？　男：我天天都喝中国茶。

　　男：What does Xiao Wang like to drink?

5) 男：方小姐，你有中文书吗？　　　女：没有，我有英文书。

　　男：What books does Miss Fang have?

6) 女：星期六是我的生日。　　　　男：我们去吃北京烤鸭，好吗？

　　男：Why are they going out for a meal?

Lesson Eight

听力练习　Listening Practice

2. Listen to the short dialogues and then choose the correct answer for each question.

1) 男：你家有几口人？　　　女：六口人。

　　男：How many people are there in her family?

2) 男：王小明是作家吗？　　女：对，他是作家。

　　男：What is Wang Xiaoming's profession?

3) 男：小李，你饿不饿？　　女：我不饿，我有点儿渴。

　　男：Is Xiao Li hungry or thirsty?

4) 男：王英有哥哥吗？　　女：王英有两个弟弟，一个妹妹，可是她没有哥哥。

　　男：What doesn't Wang Ying have?

5) 男：你家有猫吗？　　女：我有一条狗，可是我没有猫。

　　男：How many cats does she have?

6) 男：你姐姐做什么工作？　女：我姐姐是中学老师。

　　男：What does her elder sister do?

Lesson Nine

听力练习　Listening Practice

2. Listen to the short dialogues and then choose the correct answer for each question.

1) 男：你比你弟弟高吗？　　　　　女：我没有我弟弟高。
　　　男：Who is taller?

2) 男：伦敦冬天和北京一样冷吗？　女：不，伦敦比北京暖和。
　　　男：Which city is colder, Beijing or London?

3) 男：你和你姐姐谁高？　　　　　女：我姐姐比我高。
　　　男：Who is taller?

4) 男：伦敦冬天常常下雨吗？　　　女：不常下。伦敦夏天常常下雨。
　　　男：In which season does it often rain in London?

5) 男：你喜欢下雪天还是下雨天？　女：我喜欢下雪天。
　　　男：What kind of weather does the girl like?

6) 男：英国人多还是法国人多？　　女：法国人多。
　　　男：Which of these places has a bigger population?

Lesson Ten

听力练习　Listening Practice

2. Listen to the short dialogues and then choose the correct answer for each question.

1) 男：你去哪儿？　　　　　　　　女：我去商学院。
　　　男：Where is she going?

2) 男：你怎么去商学院？　　　　　女：我开车去。
　　　男：How is she going to the Business School?

3) 男：你来伦敦做什么？　　　　　女：我来看朋友。
　　　男：Why is she in London?

4) 男：你回家吗？　　　　　　　　女：我先去图书馆再回家。
　　　男：Where is she going first?

5) 男：你怎么不骑车去商店？　　　女：我没有自行车。
　　　男：Why isn't she going shopping by bike?

6) 男：小李，你明天怎么不坐火车来？女：坐火车比坐公共汽车贵多了。
　　　男：Why is Xiao Li coming by bus?

附录四 Appendix 4

练习答案　Keys to the Exercises

Lesson One

听力练习　Listening Practice

1. Listen to the recording and then choose the phrase you have heard in each group.

  1) c;   2) a;   3) a;   4) c;   5) c;   6) b

认读练习　Matching Exercise

再见	nín hǎo	sixteen
你好	zàijiàn	I am very well
十六	bāshíqī	goodbye
你好吗	wǒ hěn hǎo	eighty seven
不谢	nǐ hǎo ma	hello
九十九	bú xiè	how are you
您好	jiǔshíjiǔ	fifty two
八十七	shíliù	how do you do
我很好	nǐ hǎo	not at all
五十二	wǔshí'èr	ninety nine

Lesson Two

拼音练习　Pinyin Practice

3. Listen to the recording and then circle the Pinyin you have heard in each group.

  1) jiāo   2) nián   3) cī   4) chāng

  5) kǎo   6) nán   7) shī   8) yuè

听力练习　Listening Practice

Listen to the short dialogues and then mark each of the following sentences as true (T) or false (F).

  1. T;   2. F;   3. F;   4. T;   5. F;   6. F

语法练习　Grammar Practice

1. Rewrite the following sentences in both negative and general question forms.

  1) a. 我不叫李小英。   b. 你叫李小英吗？

  2) a. 我也不姓王。   b. 你也姓王吗？

  3) a. 他不叫方国伦。   b. 他叫方国伦吗？

4) a. 他不叫王京。 b. 他叫王京吗？

5) a. 她不姓方。 b. 她姓方吗？

6) a. 她不叫李国英。 b. 她叫李国英吗？

2. Complete the following dialogues by filling in the blanks with the appropriate words given below.

1) A. 您贵<u>姓</u>? 2) A. 你叫<u>什么</u>名字?

3) B. <u>不</u>，她不姓王。 4) B. 我<u>也</u>姓李。

5) A. 我叫方国伦，你<u>呢</u>? 6) B. <u>对</u>，他叫王京。

认读练习 Matching Exercise

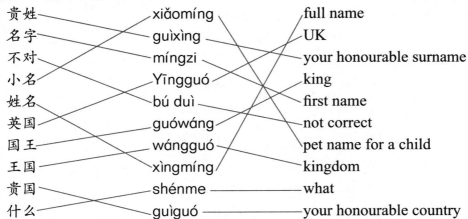

贵姓 — guìxìng — your honourable surname

名字 — míngzi — first name

不对 — bú duì — not correct

小名 — xiǎomíng — pet name for a child

姓名 — xìngmíng — full name

英国 — Yīngguó — UK

国王 — guówáng — king

王国 — wángguó — kingdom

贵国 — guìguó — your honourable country

什么 — shénme — what

翻译练习 Translation

1. 您贵姓？

2. 我叫王英，你叫什么(名字)？

3. 他叫什么(名字)？

4. 她也姓李。

5. 你叫方国伦吗？ 不，我不叫方国伦。

6. 你叫什么名字？ 我叫方英。

Lesson Three

拼音练习 Pinyin Practice

3. Listen to the recoding and circle then Pinyin you have heard in each group

1) shāng 2) zǒu 3) chù 4) xiàn

5) jué 6) lǜ 7) lóng 8) luǎn

听力练习 Listening Practice

Listen to the short dialogues and mark each of the following sentences as true (T) or false (F).

1. F; 2. T; 3. F; 4. F; 5. F; 6. F

语法练习 Grammar Practice

1.Turn the following sentences into choice questions (CQ) or special questions (SW), based on the underlined words.

1) 他叫什么(名字)？ 2) 你姓什么？

3) 王小姐是什么地方人？   4) 他们的老师是不是中国人？

5) 那是谁？   6) 你们是不是医生？

2. Complete the following dialogues by filling in the blanks with the appropriate words given below.

1) A. 你是哪国人？   2) A. 他是谁？

3) A. 你们是不是伦敦人？   4) A. 她是什么地方人？

5) B. 我们不都是中国人。   6) B. 不是，他是老师。

认读练习　Matching Exercise

中医	míngrén	old people
生字	rénmíng	northerner
生人	shēngrén	new character
老人	běifāngrén	name of a person
名人	zhōngyī	north (side)
人名	lǎorén	Chinese medicine
北方	shēngzì	famous people
北方人	běifāng	stranger
姐姐	zhōngyī yīshēng	doctor of traditional Chinese medicine
中医医生	jiějie	elder sister

翻译练习　Translation

1. 你是哪国人？

2. 他是谁？他就是王老师。

3. 这是方小姐，她也是北京人。

4. 那是李先生，他是医生。

5. 我们都是英国人。

6. 他们都不是医生。

Lesson Four

拼音练习　Pinyin Practice

3. Listen to the recording and then circle the Pinyin you have heard in each group.

1) qīn   2) xīn   3) róu   4) móu

5) niǎo   6) xiǎo   7) xùn   8) jùn

听力练习　Listening Practice

Listen to the short dialogues and choose the correct answer for each question.

1. a) 十月一号   2. c) 二月十七日   3. c) 星期三

4. c) 中国人   5. a) 六月二十九号   6. c) 我弟弟的

语法练习　Grammar Practice

1. Ask questions about the underlined parts in the following sentences.

1) 你的生日是九月几号？

2) 你妹妹今年几岁？

3) 今天(是)星期六，明天(是)星期几？

4) 后天是谁的生日？

5) 哪天是小李的生日？

6) 王老师是(中国)什么地方人？

2. Complete the following dialogues by filling in the blanks with appropriate words given below.

1) B. 我的生日是三月六号。   2) A. 你弟弟几岁？

3) A. 明天是你的生日吗？   4) A. 她多大？

5) B. 明天七号。   6) A. 今天星期几？

认读练习　Matching Exercise

年年	míngxīng	elderly people
明月	suìyuè	time
明星	zhōngniánrén	everyone
老年人	míngyuè	medium size
中年人	niánnián	star (celebrity)
大号	lǎoniánrén	middle-aged people
小号	dàhào	bright moon
岁月	rénrén	every year
人人	zhōnghào	large size
中号	xiǎohào	small size

翻译练习　Translation

1. 今天几号？

2. 今天是你的生日，生日快乐！

3. 你多大？（你几岁？）

4. 今年是2011年。明年是2012年。

5. 明天星期几？ 明天星期六。

6. 他是谁？ 他是我妹妹的老师。

Lesson Five

拼音练习　Pinyin Practice

3. Listen and then circle the Pinyin you have heard in each group.

1) dìtóu   2) dàlóu   3) sàngshī   4) shǒushì

5) Chángchéng   6) chánglóng   7) jiǎn fà   8) jiǎng huà

听力练习　Listening Practice

Listen to the short dialogues and mark each of the following sentences as true (T) or false (F).

1. F;   2. F;   3. T;   4. F;   5. T;   6. T

语法练习　Grammar Practice

1. Please place the words provided in the brackets in the correct place in each sentence.

1) 英国人(都)喝英国茶吗？

2) 你(今天晚上)看电视吗？

3) 她(天天)上网。

4) 我们(不)学英国文学。

5) 他不喝中国茶，我(也)不喝中国茶。

6) 这是谁(的)茶？

2. Complete the following dialogues by filling in the blanks with the appropriate words given below.

1) B. 我学<u>中文</u>。　　　　2) A. 你晚上<u>都</u>做什么？

3) B. 我<u>写</u>汉字。　　　　4) A. 你看中文书<u>还是</u>看英文书？

5) B. <u>喝</u>。　　　　　　　6) A. 你晚上<u>上网</u>吗？

认读练习　Matching Exercise

奶牛	zhōngxué	dairy cow
奶茶	Rìwén	middle school
电网	nǎichá	students
日文	dàxué	university
小学	nǎiniú	tea with milk
中学	diànwǎng	primary school
大学	xuésheng	Japanese (language)
学生	xiǎoxué	electricity grid
一星期	shàngxué	go to school
上学	yì xīngqī	one whole week

翻译练习　Translation

1. 你学什么专业？我学英国文学。

2. 你星期六做什么？

3. 你喝茶还是喝牛奶？

4. 王小姐天天晚上都写汉字。

5. 我早上不喝中国茶。

6. 你晚上看书还是看电视？

Lesson Six

听力练习　Listening Practice

2. Listen to the short statements or dialogues and then mark each of the following sentences as true (T) or false (F).

1) T;　　2) T;　　3) F;　　4) T;　　5) T;　　6) F

语法练习　Grammar Practice

1.Match the following verbs with the given verbs (verbs may be used more than once).

1) <u>学</u>/说汉语　　　2) <u>踢</u>足球　　　　3) <u>打</u>网球

4) <u>看</u>电视　　　　5) <u>学</u>/写汉字　　　6) <u>上</u>网

7) <u>喝</u>中国茶　　　8) <u>喝</u>咖啡　　　　9) <u>学</u>/说法语

10) <u>喝</u>牛奶　　　11) <u>看</u>/写中文书　　12) <u>看</u>老师

2. Complete the following sentences by filling in the blanks with the appropriate words given below.

1) 我会说<u>一点儿</u>英语。

2) 我们今天<u>打</u>网球，好吗？

3) 她会说汉语，<u>可是</u>她不认识汉字。

4) 你想学<u>踢</u>足球吗？

5) 我<u>喜欢</u>上网，可是我太太不喜欢上网。

6) 我们都<u>会</u>说英语。

认读练习　Matching Exercise

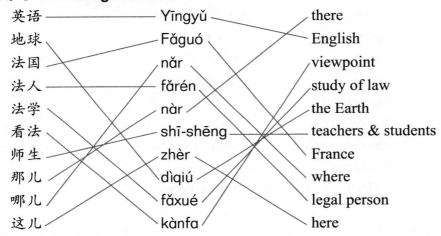

英语	Yīngyǔ	there
地球	Fǎguó	English
法国	nǎr	viewpoint
法人	fǎrén	study of law
法学	nàr	the Earth
看法	shī-shēng	teachers & students
师生	zhèr	France
那儿	dìqiú	where
哪儿	fǎxué	legal person
这儿	kànfa	here

翻译练习　Translation

1. 我的中文老师不喜欢踢足球。

2. 她不会说法语，可是她会说日语。

3. 我想学汉字。

4. 李医生会说一点儿英语。

5. 他天天晚上上网。

6. 我想喝点儿中国茶。

Lesson Seven

听力练习　Listening Practice

2. Listen to the short dialogues and circle the correct answer for each question

1) c. stir-fried rice　　2) a. British beer　　　3) b. braised meat in sauce

4) c. Chinese tea　　　5) c. English books　　6) a. her birthday

语法练习　Grammar Practice

1.Choose the correct word from a, b or c to complete each of the following sentences.

1) c. 盘　　　　　2) a. 不　　　　　3) a. 杯

4) c. 要　　　　　5) b. 没　　　　　6) b. 好吃

2. Use 没 and 不 to change the following sentences into their negative forms.

1)　今天我们没有烤鸭。

2)　我不要日本啤酒。

3)　你不喜欢踢足球吗？

4)　他们没有中国茶。

5)　他不天天看电视。

6)　我们今天晚上不写汉字。

认读练习　Matching Exercise

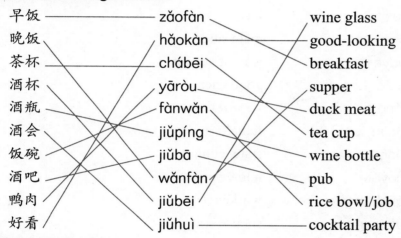

早饭　———　zǎofàn　　　　wine glass
晚饭　　　　hǎokàn　　　　good-looking
茶杯　　　　chábēi　　　　breakfast
酒杯　　　　yāròu　　　　supper
酒瓶　　　　fànwǎn　　　　duck meat
酒会　　　　jiǔpíng　　　　tea cup
饭碗　　　　jiǔbā　　　　wine bottle
酒吧　　　　wǎnfàn　　　　pub
鸭肉　　　　jiǔbēi　　　　rice bowl/job
好看　　　　jiǔhuì　　　　cocktail party

翻译练习　Translation

1. 你们有中国啤酒吗？我想要一杯。

2. 今天我们没有牛肉炒青菜。

3. 明天是我的生日。我们吃中国饭好吗？

4. 我喜欢喝中国啤酒，吃北京烤鸭。

5. 我们想要四瓶法国红酒。

6. 我很喜欢吃法国饭，法国饭很好吃。

Lesson Eight

听力练习　Listening Practice

2. Listen to the short dialogues and choose the correct answer for each question.

1) a. 六口　　　　2) b. 作家　　　　3) a. 渴

4) c. 哥哥　　　　5) c. 没有　　　　6) b. 中学老师

语法练习　Grammar Practice

1. Choose the correct word from a, b or c to complete each of the following sentences.

　1) c. 不　　　　　2) a. 两个　　　　　3) b. 有点儿

　4) b. 只　　　　　5) b. 做　　　　　6) c. 和

2. Fill in the blank with an appropriate word to complete each sentence.

　1. 他姐姐<u>是</u>中学老师。

　2. 医生今天不<u>太</u>忙。

　3. 我很累，<u>也</u>很渴。

　4. 小李的哥哥<u>也/没</u>有女朋友。

　5. 你<u>做</u>什么工作？

　6. 李明的妈妈有两<u>条</u>狗。

认读练习　Matching Exercise

说法 ——————— shuōfa　　　　　idea
想法　　　　 àirén　　　　　male student
做法　　　　 zuòyè　　　　　way of saying
国家　　　　 zuòfǎ　　　　　good friend
好友　　　　 xiǎngfǎ　　　　way of doing
爱人　　　　 guójiā　　　　　female student
男生　　　　 gōngrén　　　　state, country
女生　　　　 hǎoyǒu　　　　homework
作业　　　　 nánshēng　　　worker
工人　　　　 nǚshēng　　　　spouse

翻译练习　Translation

　1. 你爸爸妈妈(都)做什么(工作)？

　2. 王太太有两只猫、(or 和)三条狗。

　3. 我今天有点儿忙。

　4. 他家有五口人。

　5. 我不饿，也不渴。

　6. 李小英24岁。她有两个姐姐，一个弟弟和三个妹妹。

Lesson Nine

听力练习　Listening Practice

2. Listen to the short dialogues and then choose the correct answer for each question.

　1) b. 我弟弟高　　2) a. 北京冷　　3) a. 她姐姐高

　4) c. 夏天　　　　5) c. 下雪天　　6) a. 法国

语法练习　Grammar Practice

1. Choose the correct word from a, b or c to complete each of the following sentences.

　　1) c. 还　　　　2) b. 比　　　　3) a. 没有

　　4) b. 多　　　　5) c. 一样　　　6) a. 大两岁

2. Use the given information to make up sentences using comparison.

　　1) 夏天比春天热。　　　　　2) 中国比法国大。

　　3) 北京冬天比伦敦冬天冷。　4) 伦敦春天比伦敦冬天漂亮。

　　5) 中国菜比/没英国菜好吃。　6) 我比我哥哥小。

认读练习　Matching Exercise

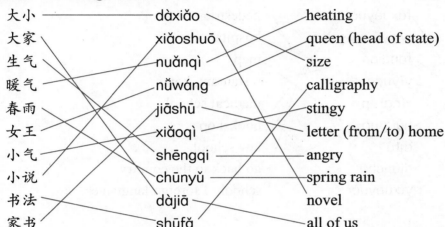

大小	dàxiǎo	heating
大家	xiǎoshuō	queen (head of state)
生气	nuǎnqì	size
暖气	nǚwáng	calligraphy
春雨	jiāshū	stingy
女王	xiǎoqì	letter (from/to) home
小气	shēngqi	angry
小说	chūnyǔ	spring rain
书法	dàjiā	novel
家书	shūfǎ	all of us

翻译练习　Translation

　　1. 中国比英国大。

　　2. 我很喜欢春天。春天不冷不热。

　　3. 我和我男朋友一样高。

　　4. 他很高。他弟弟比他还高。

　　5. 烤鸭比牛肉炒青菜贵。

　　6. 伦敦冬天天气怎么样？伦敦冬天比北京暖和多了。

Lesson Ten

听力练习　Listening Practice

2. Listen to the short dialogues and then choose the correct answer for each question.

　　1) c. 商学院　　　2) c. 开车　　　　3) c. 看朋友

　　4) a. 图书馆　　　5) b. 没有自行车　6) b. 坐火车贵

语法练习　Grammar Practice

1. Choose the correct word form a, b or c to complete each of the following sentences.

　　1) b. 坐　2) a. 还书　3) c. 回　4) a. 走　5) c. 怎么　6) b. 来

2. Using appropriate question words to ask questions to the underlined parts of the following sentences.

　　1) <u>谁</u>明天开车去商学院看朋友？

　　2) 他<u>哪天</u>开车去商学院看朋友？

　　3) 他明天<u>怎么</u>去商学院看朋友？

　　4) 他明天开车去<u>哪儿</u>看朋友？

　　5) 他明天开车去商学院<u>做什么</u>？

　　6) 他明天开车去商学院看<u>谁</u>？

认读练习　Matching Exercise

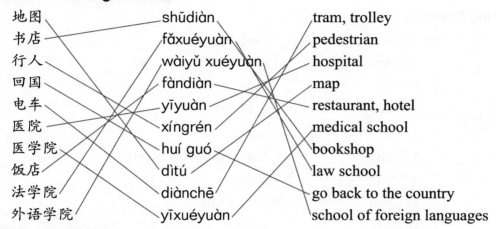

地图	shūdiàn	tram, trolley
书店	fǎxuéyuàn	pedestrian
行人	wàiyǔ xuéyuàn	hospital
回国	fàndiàn	map
电车	yīyuàn	restaurant, hotel
医院	xíngrén	medical school
医学院	huí guó	bookshop
饭店	dìtú	law school
法学院	diànchē	go back to the country
外语学院	yīxuéyuàn	school of foreign languages

翻译练习　Translation

　　1. 我明天不开车去学院。

　　2. 你去哪儿？我去图书馆还书。

　　3. 李先生今天坐地铁回家。

　　4. 他天天去图书馆看书。

　　5. 我妈妈不会骑自行车，她天天坐(公共汽)车去上班。

　　6. 王明明天不来上班，他今天晚上去北京。

附录五 Appendix 5

词汇表 A　Chinese-English Vocabulary List

爱	ài	*v*	love	8
吧	ba	*p.t*	an interrogative or suggestive particle	4
八	bā	*num*	eight	1
爸	bà	*n*	dad	8
爸爸	bàba	*n*	dad	8
白	bái	*adj*	white	7
白菜	báicài	*n*	Chinese cabbage	7
白酒	báijiǔ	*n*	white spirits	7
班	bān	*n*	shift; class	10
杯	bēi	*m.w/n*	glass of, cup of; cup	7
北	běi	*n*	north	3
北京	Běijīng	*p.n*	Beijing	3
比	bǐ	*v/prep*	compare; compared with	9
不	bù	*adv*	no, not	1
菜	cài	*n*	vegetable; dish; food	7
茶	chá	*n*	tea	5
常	cháng	*adv*	often	9
常常	chángcháng	*adv*	often	9
炒	chǎo	*v*	stir fry	7
炒饭	chǎofàn	*n*	stir-fried rice	7
车	chē	*n*	vehicle	10
吃	chī	*v*	eat	7
春	chūn	*n*	spring	9
春天	chūntiān	*n*	spring	9
打	dǎ	*v*	play (games); hit	6
打的	dǎ dí	*v-o*	take a taxi	10
大	dà	*adj*	big; old (age)	4
大学	dàxué	*n*	university	5
道	dào	*n*	way, method	4
的	de	*pt*	an attributive and possessive particle	4
地	dì	*n*	place; earth	3

地方	dìfang	*n*	place	3
地铁	dìtiě	*n*	underground	10
弟	dì	*n*	younger brother	4
弟弟	dìdi	*n*	younger brother	4
点	diǎn	*n/v*	point; hour; order	6, 7
店	diàn	*n*	shop	10
电	diàn	*n/adj*	electricity, electric	5
电视	diànshì	*n*	TV	5
东	dōng	*n*	east	10
东方	Dōngfāng	*n*	the East, the Orient	10
冬	dōng	*n*	winter	9
冬天	dōngtiān	*n*	winter	9
都	dōu	*adv*	all, both	3
对	duì	*v*	correct; right	2
对不起	duìbuqǐ	*i.e*	sorry, pardon, excuse me	4
敦*	dūn		honest	3
多	duō	*q.w/adj*	how many/much	4
饿	è	*adj*	hungry	8
儿	er		non-syllabic suffix	6
二	èr	*num*	two	1
法	fǎ	*n*	France; law; method	6
法国	Fǎguó	*p.n*	France	7
法语	Fǎyǔ	*n*	French (language)	6
饭	fàn	*n*	cooked rice; food; meal	7
方	Fāng	*n*	Fang (a surname); place	2
方国伦	Fāng Guólún	*pn*	Fang Guolun (a name)	2
该	gāi	*m.v*	should	6
高	gāo	*adj*	tall (person or building), high	9
哥	gē	*n*	elder brother	8
哥哥	gēge	*n*	elder brother	8
个	gè	*m.w*	a general measure word	7
个子	gèzi	*n*	(of a human being) height; stature	9
公	gōng	*adj*	public	10
公共	gōnggòng	*adj*	public	10
公共汽车	gōnggòng qìchē	*n*	bus	10

工	gōng	*n/v*	work, labour	8
工作	gōngzuò	*n/v*	work	8
共	gòng	*adv*	together	10
狗	gǒu	*n*	dog	8
馆	guǎn	*n*	building	10
贵	guì	*adj*	honourable; expensive	2
国	guó	*n*	country	2
还	hái	*adv*	still	5
还是	háishi	*conj*	or (for question)	5
汉	Hàn	*n*	Chinese	5
汉语	Hànyǔ	*n*	Chinese language	6
汉字	Hànzì	*n*	Chinese character	5
好	hǎo	*adj*	good; well	1
好吃	hǎochī	*adj*	delicious	7
号	hào	*n*	day; number; size	4
喝	hē	*v*	drink	5
和	hé	*conj*	and	5
很	hěn	*adv*	very, rather	1
红	hóng	*adj*	red	7
红酒	hóngjiǔ	*n*	red wine	7
红烧肉	hóngshāoròu	*n*	braised meat in soy sauce	7
后	hòu		behind, after	4
后天	hòutiān		the day after tomorrow	4
欢*	huān		happy	6
还	huán	*v*	return	10
还书	huán shū	*v-o*	return books	10
回	huí	*v*	go back, return	10
回家	huí jiā	*v-o*	go back home	10
会	huì	*m.v/n*	can, may; meeting	6
火	huǒ	*n*	fire	10
火车	huǒchē	*n*	train	10
几	jǐ	*q.w*	how many (less than 10); several	4
纪*	jì	*n*	age	4
加	jiā	*conj*	and	5
家	jiā	*n/m.w*	home; family; house; specialist in a field	8

附录五 Appendix 5

见	jiàn	*v*	see; meet	1
叫	jiào	*v*	be called; call, shout	2
姐	jiě	*n*	elder sister	3
姐姐	jiějie	*n*	elder sister	3
今	jīn	*n*	today, this	4
今年	jīnnián	*n*	this year	4
今天	jīntiān	*n*	today	4
京*	jīng	*n*	capital	2
九	jiǔ	*num*	nine	1
九月	jiǔyuè	*t.w*	September	4
酒	jiǔ	*n*	alcoholic drink	7
就	jiù	*adv*	exactly	3
咖啡	kāfēi	*n*	coffee	5
开	kāi	*v*	drive; open	10
开车	kāi chē	*v-o*	drive	10
看	kàn	*v*	see, watch, look; read	5
烤	kǎo	*v*	roast; bake	7
烤鸭	kǎoyā	*n*	roast duck	7
可	kě	*m.v*	may, can	6
可爱	kě'ài	*adj*	lovely	8
可是	kěshì	*conj*	but	6
渴	kě	*adj*	thirsty	8
客气	kèqi	*adj*	polite, couteous	1
口	kǒu	*m.w/n*	m.w for family members; mouth	8
快	kuài	*adj/adv*	pleased; fast	4,10
快乐	kuàilè	*adj*	happy	4
来	lái	*v*	come (the opposite direction of 去)	10
篮	lán	*n*	basket	9
篮球	lánqiú	*n*	basketball	9
老	lǎo	*adj*	old	3
老师	lǎoshī	*n*	teacher	3
了	le	*pt*	part of a complement	7
乐	lè	*adj*	happy	4
累	lèi	*adj*	tired	8
冷	lěng	*adj*	cold	9

李	Lǐ	*n*	Li (a surname); plum	2
李贵	Lǐ Guì	*p.n*	Li Gui (a name)	2
李小英	Lǐ Xiǎoyīng	*p.n*	Li Xiaoying (a name)	2
李月明	Lǐ Yuèmíng	*p.n*	Li Yueming (a name)	2
两	liǎng	*num*	two (use in front of a measure word)	8
亮	liàng	*adj*	bright, shiny	9
六	liù	*num*	six	1
路	lù	*n*	road	10
律	lǜ	*n*	law; rule	8
律师	lǜshī	*n*	lawyer	8
伦*	lún	*n*	ethics	2
伦敦	Lúndūn	*p.n*	London	3
伦敦大学	Lúndūn Dàxué	*p.n*	University of London	5
吗	ma	*pt*	an interrogative particle	1
妈	mā	*n*	mum	8
妈妈	māma	*n*	mum	8
忙	máng	*adj*	busy	8
猫	māo	*n*	cat	8
么*	me		what	2
没	méi	*adv*	negation word for 有	7
妹	mèi	*n*	younger sister	4
妹妹	mèimei	*n*	younger sister	4
们*	men		plural suffix of human beings	3
名	míng	*n*	name	2
名字	míngzi	*n*	name	2
明	míng	*n*	next; bright	2, 3
明天	míngtiān	*t.w*	tomorrow	4
那	nà/nèi	*pron*	that	3
哪	nǎ/něi	*adv*	which	3
哪儿	nǎr	*q.w*	where	10
奶	nǎi	*n*	milk	5
男	nán	*n*	man, male	8
男朋友	nán péngyou	*n*	boyfriend	8
呢	ne	*pt*	interrogative particle for follow-up questions	2
你	nǐ	*pron*	you	1

你们	nǐmen	pron	you (plural)	3
年	nián	n	year	4
年纪	niánjì	n	age	4
您	nín	pron	you (polite form)	1
牛	niú	n	cow, bull	5
牛奶	niúnǎi	n	(cow) milk	5
牛肉	niúròu	n	beef	7
女	nǚ	n	woman	8
女朋友	nǚ péngyou	n	girlfriend	8
暖	nuǎn	adj	warm	9
暖和	nuǎnhuo	adj	warm	9
盘	pán	m.w/n	dish of, plate of; plate	7
胖	pàng	adj	stout; fat	9
朋*	péng	n	friend	8
朋友	péngyou	n	friend	8
啤*	pí		beer	7
啤酒	píjiǔ	n	beer	7
漂*	piào	adj	smart	9
漂亮	piàoliang	adj	pretty	9
瓶	píng	m.w/n	bottle of; bottle	7
七	qī	num	seven	1
期	qī	n	period	4
骑	qí	v	ride (a bicycle, horse etc.)	10
起*	qǐ	v	rise	4
气	qì	n	air; breath	9
汽	qì	n	steam	10
汽车	qìchē	n	automobile, car	10
青	qīng	adj	green	7
青菜	qīngcài	n	green vegetable	7
青青	Qīngqing	p.n	Qingqing (a name)	9
秋	qiū	n	autumn	9
秋天	qiūtiān	n	autumn	9
球	qiú	n	ball	6
去	qù	v	go	10
热	rè	adj	hot	9

人	rén	*n*	person, people	3
认	rèn	*v*	recognise	6
认识	rènshi	*v*	know	6
日	rì	*n*	day (formal); sun	4
日语	Rìyǔ	*n*	Japanese (language)	6
肉	ròu	*n*	meat	7
三	sān	*num*	three	1
商	shāng	*n/adj*	business; commercial	8
商店	shāngdiàn	*n*	shop	10
商人	shāngrén	*n*	businessman	8
上	shàng	*prep/v*	go (online); on	5
上班	shàngbān	*v/n*	go to work	10
上海	Shànghǎi	*p.n*	Shanghai	3
上网	shàng wǎng	*v*	surf the Internet	5
商学院	shāngxuéyuàn	*n*	business school	10
烧	shāo	*v*	cook; braise	7
少	shǎo	*adj*	few; little	9
什*	shén		what	2
生	shēng	*n/v*	a person; be born	3
生日	shēngrì	*n*	birthday	4
什么	shénme	*q.w*	what	2
师	shī	*n*	master	3
识	shí	*v*	know	6
十	shí	*num*	ten	1
十一月	shíyīyuè	*t.w*	November	4
是	shì	*v*	be	3
视	shì	*n/v*	vision; watch	5
瘦	shòu	*adj*	thin (a person)	9
书	shū	*n*	book	5
谁	shuí/shéi	*q.w*	who	3
说	shuō	*v/n*	speak	6
四	sì	*num*	four	1
岁	suì	*m.w/n*	year (age); time	4
他	tā	*pron*	he; him	2
他们	tāmen	*pron*	they; them	3

她	tā	*pron*	she; her	2
太	tài	*n/adv*	wife; too (excessively)	3
太太	tàitai	*n*	Mrs; wife	3
踢	tī	*v*	kick; play (football)	6
天	tiān	*n*	day; sky	4
天气	tiānqì	*n*	weather	9
天天	tiāntiān	*adv*	every day	5
条	tiáo	*m.w*	m.w for various long narrow things	8
铁	tiě	*n*	iron	10
图	tú	*n*	map; picture	10
图书馆	túshūguǎn	*n*	library	10
外	wài	*n*	outside; foreign	6
外语	wàiyǔ	*n*	foreign language	6
碗	wǎn	*m.w/n*	bowl of; bowl	7
晚	wǎn	*adj*	late	5
晚上	wǎnshang	*t.w*	evening	5
王	Wáng	*n*	Wang (a surname); king	2
王京	Wáng Jīng	*p.n*	Wang Jing (Jim King) (a name)	2
网	wǎng	*n*	net	5
网球	wǎngqiú	*n*	tennis	6
为	wèi	*prep*	for, on account of	6
为什么	wèishénme	*q.w*	why	6
文	wén	*n*	written language	5
文学	wénxué	*n*	literature	5
我	wǒ	*pron*	I; me	1
我们	wǒmen	*pron*	we; us	3
五	wǔ	*num*	five	1
五星啤酒	Wǔxīng Píjiǔ	*p.n*	Five Stars Beer	7
喜*	xǐ		like	6
喜欢	xǐhuan	*v*	like	6
下	xià	*v*	fall; get off	9
下雪	xià xuě	*v-o*	snow	9
下雨	xià yǔ	*v-o*	rain	9
夏	xià	*n*	summer	9
夏天	xiàtiān	*n*	summer	9

先	xiān	*adv*	first	3
先生	xiānsheng	*n*	Mr; husband	3
想	xiǎng	*m.v*	would like to, intend; think; miss	6
小	xiǎo	*adj*	small; young	2
小姐	xiǎojiě	*n*	Miss	3
写	xiě	*v*	write	5
谢	xiè	*v/n*	thank; Xie (a surname)	1
星	xīng	*n*	star	4
星期	xīngqī	*n*	week	4
星期二	xīngqī'èr	*t.w*	Tuesday	4
行	xíng	*v*	walk	10
姓	xìng	*v*	be surnamed	2
学	xué	*v/n*	learn, study	5
学生	xuésheng	*n*	student	5
学院	xuéyuàn	*n*	college	10
雪	xuě	*v*	snow	9
鸭	yā	*n*	duck	7
样*	yàng	*m.w/n*	type; manner	9
要	yào	*v/m.v*	want	6
也	yě	*adv*	also, too; neither	2
业	yè	*n*	course; industry	5
一	yī	*num*	one	1
一点儿	yìdiǎnr	*n/adj*	a bit	6
一起	yìqǐ	*adv*	together	6
一样	yíyàng	*adj/adv*	the same	9
医	yī	*n/v*	medicine; to cure	3
医生	yīshēng	*n*	doctor	3
因	yīn	*n*	cause, reason for	6
因为	yīnwèi	*conj*	because	6
应	yīng	*m.v*	should	6
应该	yīnggāi	*m.v*	should	6
英*	yīng	*n*	hero; Britain	2
英国	Yīngguó	*p.n*	UK	3
英文	Yīngwén	*n*	English (language)	5
友*	yǒu	*n*	friend	8

有	yǒu	*v*	have, there be	7
有点儿	yǒudiǎnr	*adv*	somewhat; a bit	8
有名	yǒumíng	*adj*	famous	7
语	yǔ	*n*	language	6
雨	yǔ	*n*	rain	9
院	yuàn	*n*	compound, courtyard	10
月	yuè	*n*	month, moon	2
再	zài	*adv*	again; later	1
再见	zàijiàn	*exp*	bye, see you again	1
早	zǎo	*adj*	early	5
早上	zǎoshang	*t.w*	morning	5
怎*	zěn		how; why	9
怎么	zěnme	*adv*	how	10
怎么样	zěnmeyàng	*q.w*	how is it?	9
这	zhè/zhèi	*pron*	this	3
这儿	zhèr	*l.w*	here	8
只	zhī	*m.w*	m.w for birds and some other animals	7
知道	zhīdào	*v*	know	4
只	zhǐ	*adv*	only	7
中	zhōng	*n*	middle	3
中国	Zhōngguó	*p.n*	China	3
中文	Zhōngwén	*n*	Chinese (language)	5
专	zhuān	*adj*	specialised	5
专业	zhuānyè	*n*	major, subject	5
子*	zi		a noun suffix	9
自*	zì		self, auto	10
自行车	zìxíngchē	*n*	bike	10
字	zì	*n*	character	2
走	zǒu	*v*	walk	10
走路	zǒu lù	*v-o*	walk	10
足	zú	*n*	foot	6
足球	zúqiú	*n*	football	6
做	zuò	*v*	make, do	5
坐	zuò	*v*	sit; take (bus etc.)	10
作	zuò	*v*	do; make; write	8
作家	zuòjiā	*n*	writer	8

附录六　Appendix 6

词汇表 B　English-Chinese Vocabulary List

a bit; a bit of	一点儿	yìdiǎnr	*n*	6
a general measure word	个	gè	*m.w*	7
a person; be born	生	shēng	*n/v*	3
again; later	再	zài	*adv*	1
age	年纪	niánjì	*n*	4
air; breath	气	qì	*n*	9
alcoholic drink	酒	jiǔ	*n*	7
all, both	都	dōu	*adv*	3
also, too; neither	也	yě	*adv*	2
an attributive and possessive particle	的	de	*pt*	4
an interrogative or suggestive particle	吧	ba	*pt*	4
an interrogative particle	吗	ma	*pt*	1
and	和	hé	*conj*	5
automobile	汽车	qìchē	*n*	10
autumn	秋	qiū	*n*	9
autumn	秋天	qiūtiān	*n*	9
ball	球	qiú	*n*	9
basket	篮	lán	*n*	9
basketball	篮球	lánqiú	*n*	6
be	是	shì	*v*	3
be called; call, shout	叫	jiào	*v*	2
be surnamed	姓	xìng	*v*	2
because	因为	yīnwèi	*conj*	6
beef	牛肉	niúròu	*n*	7
beer	啤*	pí		7
beer	啤酒	píjiǔ	*n*	7
Beijing	北京	Běijīng	*p.n*	3
big; old (age)	大	dà	*adj*	4
bike	自行车	zìxíngchē	*n*	10
birthday	生日	shēngrì	*n*	4
book	书	shū	*n*	5

bottle of; bottle	瓶	píng	m.w/n	7
bowl of; bowl	碗	wǎn	m.w/n	7
boyfriend	男朋友	nán péngyou	n	8
braised meat in soy sauce	红烧肉	hóngshāoròu	n	7
bright, shiny	亮	liàng	adj	9
building	馆	guǎn	n	10
bus	公共汽车	gōnggòng qìchē	n	10
business school	商学院	shāngxuéyuàn	n	10
business; commercial	商	shāng	n/adj	8
businessman	商人	shāngrén	n	8
busy	忙	máng	adj	8
but	可是	kěshì	conj	6
bye, see you again	再见	zàijiàn	exp	1
can, may; meeting	会	huì	m.v/n	6
capital	京*	jīng	n	2
cat	猫	māo	n	8
cause, reason for	因	yīn	n	6
character	字	zì	n	2
China	中国	Zhōngguó	p.n	3
Chinese	汉	Hàn	n	5
Chinese cabbage	白菜	báicài	n	7
Chinese character	汉字	Hànzì	n	5
Chinese (language)	中文	Zhōngwén	n	5
Chinese (language)	汉语	Hànyǔ	n	6
coffee	咖啡	kāfēi	n	4
cold	冷	lěng	adj	9
college	学院	xuéyuàn	n	10
come (the opposite direction of 去)	来	lái	v	10
compare; compared with	比	bǐ	v/prep	9
compound, courtyard	院	yuàn	n	10
cook; braise	烧	shāo	v	7
cooked rice; food, meal	饭	fàn	n	7
correct; right	对	duì	v	2
country	国	guó	n	2
course, industry	业	yè	n	5

cow, bull	牛	niú	*n*	5
(cow) milk	牛奶	niúnǎi	*n*	5
dad	爸	bà	*n*	8
dad	爸爸	bàba	*n*	8
day (formal); sun	日	rì	*n*	4
day; sky	天	tiān	*n*	4
day; number; size	号	hào	*n*	4
(the) day after tomorrow	后天	hòutiān	*n*	4
delicious	好吃	hǎochī	*adj*	7
dish of, plate of; plate	盘	pán	*m.w/n*	7
do; make; write	作	zuò	*v*	8
doctor	医生	yīshēng	*n*	3
dog	狗	gǒu	*n*	8
drink	喝	hē	*v*	5
drive	开车	kāi chē	*v-o*	10
drive; open; have a meeting	开	kāi	*v*	10
duck	鸭	yā	*n*	7
early	早	zǎo	*adj*	5
east	东	dōng	*n*	10
eat	吃	chī	*v*	7
eight	八	bā	*num*	1
elder brother	哥	gē	*n*	8
elder brother	哥哥	gēge	*n*	8
elder sister	姐	jiě	*n*	3
elder sister	姐姐	jiějie	*n*	3
electricity; electric	电	diàn	*n/adj*	5
English (language)	英文	Yīngwén	*n*	5
ethics	伦*	lún	*n*	2
evening	晚上	wǎnshang	*t.w*	5
every day	天天	tiāntiān	*adv*	5
exactly	就	jiù	*adv*	3
fall; get off	下	xià	*v*	9
famous	有名	yǒumíng	*adj*	7
Fang (a surname); place	方	Fāng/fāng	*p.n/n*	2
Fang Guolun (a name)	方国伦	Fāng Guólún	*p.n*	2

few; little	少	shǎo	adj	9
fire	火	huǒ	n	10
first	先	xiān	adv	3
five	五	wǔ	num	1
Five Stars Beer	五星啤酒	Wǔxīng Píjiǔ	p.n	7
foot	足	zú	n	6
football	足球	zúqiú	n	6
for, on account of	为	wèi	prep	6
foreign language	外语	wàiyǔ	n	6
four	四	sì	num	1
France	法国	Fǎguó	p.n	7
France; law; method	法	fǎ	n	6
French (language)	法语	Fǎyǔ	n	6
friend	朋友	péngyou	n	8
friend	朋*	péng	n	8
friend	友*	yǒu	n	8
girlfriend	女朋友	nǚ péngyou	n	8
glass of, cup of; cup	杯	bēi	m.w/n	7
go (opposite direction of 来)	去	qù	v	10
go back home	回家	huíjiā	v-o	10
go back, return	回	huí	v	10
go to work	上班	shàngbān	v/n	10
good; well	好	hǎo	adj	1
green	青	qīng	adj	7
green vegetable	青菜	qīngcài	n	7
happy	快乐	kuàilè	adj	4
happy	乐	lè	adj	4
happy	欢*	huān		6
have, there be	有	yǒu	v	7
he; him	他	tā	pron	2
height, stature	个子	gèzi	n	9
here	这儿	zhèr	l.w	8
hero; Britain	英*	yīng	n	2
home; family; house; specialist in a field	家	jiā	n/m.w	8
honest	敦*	dūn		3

honourable; expensive	贵	guì	*adj*	2
hot	热	rè	*adj*	9
how	怎么	zěnme	*adv*	10
how is it?	怎么样	zěnmeyàng	*q.w*	9
how many (less than 10)	几	jǐ	*q.w*	4
how many/much; many, much	多	duō	*q.w/adj*	4
how; why	怎*	zěn		9
hungry	饿	è	*adj*	8
I; me	我	wǒ	*pron*	1
interrogative particle for follow-up questions	呢	ne	*pt*	2
iron	铁	tiě	*n*	10
Japanese (language)	日语	Rìyǔ	*n*	6
kick; play (football)	踢	tī	*v*	6
know	认识	rènshi	*v*	6
know	识	shí	*v*	6
know	知	zhī	*v*	4
know	知道	zhīdào	*v*	4
language	语	yǔ	*n*	6
late	晚	wǎn	*adj*	5
law; rule	律	lǜ	*n*	8
laywer	律师	lǜshī	*n*	8
learn, study	学	xué	*v/n*	5
library	图书馆	túshūguǎn	*n*	10
Li (a surname); plum	李	Lǐ	*n*	2
Li Gui (a name)	李贵	Lǐ Guì	*p.n*	2
Li Xiaoying (a name)	李小英	Lǐ Xiǎoyīng	*p.n*	2
like	喜*	xǐ		6
like	喜欢	xǐhuan	*v*	6
literature	文学	wénxué	*n*	5
London	伦敦	Lúndūn	*p.n*	3
love	爱	ài	*v*	8
lovely	可爱	kě'ài	*daj*	8
m.w for birds and some other animals	只	zhī	*m.w*	7
m.w for family members; mouth	口	kǒu	*m.w/n*	8
m.w for various long narrow things	条	tiáo	*m.w*	8

附录六 Appendix 6

major, subject	专业	zhuānyè	*n*	5
make, do	做	zuò	*v*	5
man, male	男	nán	*n*	8
map; picture	图	tú	*n*	10
master	师	shī	*n*	3
may, can	可	kě	*m.v*	6
meat	肉	ròu	*n*	7
medicine; to cure	医	yī	*n/v*	3
middle	中	zhōng	*n*	3
milk	奶	nǎi	*n*	5
Miss	小姐	xiǎojiě	*n*	3
month, moon	月	yuè	*n*	2
morning	早上	zǎoshang	*t.w*	5
Mr; husband	先生	xiānsheng	*n*	3
Mrs; wife	太太	tàitai	*n*	3
mum	妈	mā	*n*	8
mum	妈妈	māma	*n*	8
name	名	míng	*n*	2
name	名字	míngzi	*n*	2
negation word for 有	没	méi	*adv*	7
net	网	wǎng	*n*	5
next; bright	明	míng	*n*	4
nine	九	jiǔ	*num*	1
no, not	不	bù	*adv*	1
non-syllabic suffix	儿	er		6
north	北	běi	*n*	3
November	十一月	shíyīyuè	*t.w*	4
often	常	cháng	*adv*	9
often	常常	chángcháng	*adv*	9
old	老	lǎo	*adj*	3
go (online); on	上	shàng	*prep/v*	5
one	一	yī	*num*	1
only	只	zhǐ	*adv*	7
or (for question)	还是	háishi	*conj*	5
outside; foreign	外	wài	*n*	6

part of a complement	了	le	*pt*	7
period	期	qī	*n*	4
person, people	人	rén	*n*	3
place	地方	dìfang	*n*	3
place; earth	地	dì	*n*	3
play (games); hit	打	dǎ	*v*	6
pleased; fast	快	kuài	*adj/adv*	4, 10
plural suffix of human beings	们*	men		3
point; hour; order	点	diǎn	*n/v*	6, 7
polite, courteous	客气	kèqi	*adj*	1
pretty	漂亮	piàoliang	*adj*	9
public	公	gōng	*adj*	10
public	公共	gōnggòng	*adj*	10
rain	下雨	xiàyǔ	*v-o*	9
rain	雨	yǔ	*n*	9
recognise	认	rèn	*v*	6
red	红	hóng	*adj*	7
red wine	红酒	hóngjiǔ	*n*	7
return	还	huán	*v*	10
return books	还书	huán shū	*v-o*	10
ride (a bicycle, horse etc)	骑	qí	*v*	10
rise	起*	qǐ	*v*	4
road	路	lù	*n*	10
roast duck	烤鸭	kǎoyā	*n*	7
roast; bake	烤	kǎo	*v*	7
see, watch, look; read	看	kàn	*v*	5
see; meet	见	jiàn	*v*	1
self, auto	自*	zì		10
September	九月	jiǔyuè	*t.w*	4
seven	七	qī	*num*	1
Shanghai	上海	Shànghǎi	*p.n*	3
she; her	她	tā	*pron*	2
shift	班	bān	*n*	10
shop	商店	shāngdiàn	*n*	10
shop	店	diàn	*n*	10

should	应	yīng	*m.v*	6
should	该	gāi	*m.v*	6
should	应该	yīnggāi	*m.v*	6
sit, take (bus etc)	坐	zuò	*v*	10
six	六	liù	*num*	1
small; young	小	xiǎo	*adj*	2
smart	漂*	piào	*adj*	9
snow	下雪	xià xuě	*v-o*	9
snow	雪	xuě	*v*	9
somewhat; a bit	有点儿	yǒudiǎnr	*adv*	8
sorry, pardon, excuse me	对不起	duìbuqǐ	*i.e*	4
speak	说	shuō	*v*	6
specialised	专	zhuān	*adj*	5
spring	春	chūn	*n*	9
spring	春天	chūntiān	*n*	9
star	星	xīng	*n*	4
steam	汽	qì	*n*	10
still	还	hái	*adv*	7
stir fry	炒	chǎo	*v*	7
stir-fried rice	炒饭	chǎofàn	*n*	7
stout; fat	胖	pàng	*adj*	9
student	学生	xuésheng	*n*	8
summer	夏	xià	*n*	9
summer	夏天	xiàtiān	*n*	9
surf the Internet	上网	shàng wǎng	*v*	5
take a taxi	打的	dǎ di	*v-o*	10
tall (person or building), high	高	gāo	*adj*	9
tea	茶	chá	*n*	5
teacher	老师	lǎoshī	*n*	3
ten	十	shí	*num*	1
tennis	网球	wǎngqiú	*n*	6
thank; Xie (a surname)	谢	xiè/Xiè	*v/p.n*	1
that	那	nà/nèi	*pron*	3
the East, the Orient	东方	Dōngfāng	*n*	10
the same	一样	yíyàng	*adj/adv*	9

they; them	他们	tāmen	*pron*	3
thin (a person)	瘦	shòu	*adj*	9
thirsty	渴	kě	*adj*	8
this	这	zhè/zhèi	*pron*	3
this year	今年	jīnnián	*n*	4
three	三	sān	*num*	1
tired	累	lèi	*adj*	8
today	今天	jīntiān	*n*	4
today, this	今	jīn	*n*	4
together	一起	yìqǐ	*adv*	6
together	共	gòng	*adv*	10
tomorrow	明天	míngtiān	*t.w*	4
train	火车	huǒchē	*n*	10
Tuesday	星期二	xīngqī'èr	*t.w*	4
TV	电视	diànshì	*n*	5
two	二	èr	*num*	1
two (use in front of a measure word)	两	liǎng	*num*	8
type; manner	样*	yàng	*m.w/n*	9
UK	英国	Yīngguó	*p.n*	3
underground	地铁	dìtiě	*n*	10
University of London	伦敦大学	Lúndūn Dàxué	*p.n*	5
vegetable; dish; food	菜	cài	*n*	7
vehicle	车	chē	*n*	10
very, rather	很	hěn	*adv*	1
vision; watch	视	shì	*n/v*	5
walk	走	zǒu	*v*	10
walk	走路	zǒu lù	*v-o*	10
walk; shop	行	xíng	*v*	10
Wang (a surname); king	王	Wáng	*n*	2
Wang Jing (Jim King) (a name)	王京	Wáng Jīng	*p.n*	2
want	要	yào	*v/m.v*	6
warm	暖	nuǎn	*adj*	9
warm	暖和	nuǎnhuo	*adj*	9
way; method	道	dào	*n*	4
we; us	我们	wǒmen	*pron*	3

weather	天气	tiānqì	*n*	9
week	星期	xīngqī	*n*	4
what	么*	me		2
what	什么	shénme	*q.w*	2
what	什*	shén		2
where	哪儿	nǎr	*adv*	10
which	哪	nǎ/něi	*q.w*	3
white	白	bái	*adj*	7
white spirits	白酒	báijiǔ	*n*	7
who	谁	shuí/shéi	*q.w*	3
why	为什么	wèishénme	*q.w*	6
wife; too (excessively)	太	tài	*n/adv*	3
winter	冬	dōng	*n*	9
winter	冬天	dōngtiān	*n*	9
woman	女	nǚ	*n*	8
work	工作	gōngzuò	*n/v*	8
work, labour	工	gōng	*n/v*	8
would like to, intend; think; miss	想	xiǎng	*m.v/v*	6
write	写	xiě	*v*	5
writer	作家	zuòjiā	*n*	8
(written) language	文	wén	*n*	5
year	年	nián	*n*	4
year (age); time	岁	suì	*m.w/n*	4
you	你	nǐ	*pron*	1
you (plural)	你们	nǐmen	*pron*	3
you (polite form)	您	nín	*pron*	1
younger brother	弟	dì	*n*	4
younger brother	弟弟	dìdi	*n*	4
younger sister	妹	mèi	*n*	4
younger sister	妹妹	mèimei	*n*	4

附录七 Appendix 7

拼音文本 Pinyin Texts for the Dialogues and Readings

Lesson one Nǐ Hǎo!

Useful Expressions

A:	Nǐ hǎo!	B:	Nǐ hǎo!
A:	Nín hǎo!	B:	Nín hǎo!
A:	Nǐ hǎo ma?	B:	Wǒ hěn hǎo.
A:	Xièxie.	B:	Bú xiè.
A:	Zàijiàn!	B:	Zàijiàn!

Lesson Two Wǒ Jiào Wáng Jīng

Dialogue One

Lǐ:　　　Nín hǎo!
Wáng:　 Nín hǎo!
Lǐ:　　　Nín guì xìng?
Wáng:　 Wǒ xìng Wáng, wǒ jiào Wáng Jīng, nín ne?
Lǐ:　　　Wǒ xìng Lǐ.
Wáng:　 Nín jiào Lǐ Xiǎoyīng ma?
Lǐ:　　　Duì, wǒ jiào Lǐ Xiǎoyīng.

Dialogue Two

Wáng:　 Nǐ hǎo!
Lǐ:　　　Nǐ hǎo!
Wáng:　 Nǐ jiào shénme míngzi?
Lǐ:　　　Wǒ jiào Lǐ Guì.
Wáng:　 Wǒ jiào Wáng Jīng. Tā jiào shénme míngzi?
Lǐ:　　　Tā yě xìng Lǐ, tā jiào Lǐ Yuèmíng.
Wáng:　 Tā ne? Tā yě xìng Lǐ ma?
Lǐ:　　　Bu, tā bú xìng Lǐ, ta xìng Fāng, tā jiào Fāng Guólún.

Lesson Three Wáng Xiānsheng Shì Yīngguórén

Dialogue One

Wáng:　 Nín hǎo, wǒ jiào Wáng Jīng.
Lǐ:　　　Nín hǎo, wǒ jiào Lǐ Xiǎoyīng.
Wáng:　 Lǐ xiǎojiě shì nǎ guó rén?
Lǐ:　　　Wǒ shì Zhōngguórén.
Wáng:　 Nín shì Zhōngguó shénme dìfang rén?

| Lǐ: | Wǒ shì Běijīngrén. Wáng xiānsheng shì bu shì Yīngguórén? |
| Wáng: | Shì, wǒ shì Lúndūnrén. |

Dialogue Two

Fāng:	Wáng lǎoshī, zhè shì Lǐ xiǎojiě. Lǐ xiǎojiě, zhè shì Wáng lǎoshī.
Lǐ :	Nín hǎo, Wáng lǎoshī.
Wáng:	Nǐ hǎo, Lǐ xiǎojiě.
Fāng :	Wáng lǎoshī, Lǐ xiǎojiě yě shì Shànghǎirén.
Wáng:	Shì ma? Wǒmen dōu shì Shànghǎirén.
Fāng:	Nà shì shuí? Nà shì bu shì nín tàitai?
Wáng:	Shì, nà jiù shì wǒ tàitai.
Lǐ:	Wáng tàitai yě shì lǎoshī ma?
Wáng:	Bù, tā shì yīshēng.

Lesson Four Jīntiān Jǐ Hào?

Dialogue One

Lǐ:	Wáng Jīng, jīntiān xīngqī jǐ?
Wáng:	Jīntiān xīngqī'èr.
Lǐ:	Jīntiān jǐ hào?
Wáng:	Èrshísān hào.
Lǐ:	Jiǔyuè èrshísān hào! Míngtiān shì wǒ dìdi de shēngrì.
Wáng:	Shì ma? Tā jīnnián jǐ suì?
Lǐ:	Tā Jīntiān bā suì, míngtiān jiǔ suì.
Wáng:	Wǒ mèimei jīnnián yě jiǔ suì.
Lǐ:	Tā de shēngrì shì nǎ tiān?
Wáng:	Shíyīyuè qī hào.

Dialogue Two

Wáng:	Lǐ Yīng, nǐ de shēngrì shì jǐ yuè jǐ hào?
Lǐ:	Shíyīyuè shísì hào.
Wáng:	Shíyīyuè shísì hào? Hòutiān jiù shì shíyīyuè shísì hào ba?
Lǐ:	Duì. Hòutiān jiù shì wǒ de shēngrì.
Wáng:	Shēngrì kuàilè!
Lǐ:	Xièxie.
Wáng:	Nǐ jīnnián duō dà?
Lǐ :	Wǒ jīnnián èrshí suì. Nǐ de shēngrì shì nǎtiān?
Wáng:	Wǔ yuè liù hào.
Lǐ:	Wǔ yuè liù hào yě shì Fāng lǎoshī de shēngrì.
Wáng:	Fāng lǎoshī jīnnián duō dà niánjì?
Lǐ:	Duìbuqǐ, wǒ bù zhīdào.

Lesson Five Tā Tiāntiān Wǎnshang Dōu Xiě Hànzì

Dialogue One

| Fāng: | Nǐ hǎo, Wǒ jiào Fāng Jīng. |

Lǐ:	Nǐ hǎo, wǒ jiào Lǐ Yīng.
Fāng:	Nǐ shì xuésheng ma?
Lǐ:	Duì, wǒ shì Lúndūn Dàxué de xuésheng.
Fāng:	Nǐ xué shénme zhuānyè?
Lǐ:	Wǒ xué Zhōngwén. Nǐ ne?
Fāng:	Wǒ xué Yīngguó wénxué. Nǐ jīntiān wǎnshang zuò shénme?
Lǐ:	Wǒ xiě Hànzì.
Fāng:	Nǐ míngtiān wǎnshang zuò shénme?
Lǐ:	Wǒ xiě Hànzì.
Fāng:	Nǐ tiāntiān wǎnshang dōu xiě Hànzì ma?
Lǐ:	Duì. Nǐ wǎnshang dōu zuò shénme?
Fāng:	Wǒ kàn shū, kàn diànshì, shàng wǎng.

Dialogue Two

Lǐ:	Xiǎo Wáng, nǐ hē bu hē chá?
Wáng:	Wǒ zǎoshang bù hē, xièxie.
Lǐ:	Nǐ zǎoshang hē shénme?
Wáng:	Wǒ hē niúnǎi hé kāfēi. Nǐ hē kāfēi ma?
Lǐ:	Wǒ bù hē kāfēi, zǎoshang wǎnshang wǒ dōu hē chá.
Wáng:	Nǐ hē Zhōngguó chá háishi Yīngguó chá?
Lǐ:	Wǒ hē Zhōngguó chá.

Lesson Six　Wǒ Huì Shuō Yìdiǎnr Hànyǔ

Dialogue One

Lǐ:	Wáng Jīng, nǐ shì Yīngguórén, wèishénme yào xué Hànyǔ?
Wáng:	Wǒ xǐhuan xué wàiyǔ. Wǒ huì shuō Fǎyǔ, yě huì shuō yìdiǎnr Rìyǔ.
Lǐ:	Nǐ huì shuō Rìyǔ? Nǐ rènshi Hànzì ma?
Wáng:	Bú rènshi.
Lǐ:	Wǒ huì shuō yìdiǎnr Hànyǔ, kěshì wǒ yě bú rènshi Hànzì.
Wáng:	Nǐ xiǎng xué Hànzì ma?
Lǐ:	Wǒ de lǎoshī shuō wǒ yīnggāi xué, kěshì wǒ bù xiǎng xué.
Wáng:	Wèishénme?
Lǐ:	Wǒ xǐhuan Hànzì, kěshì Hànzì bù xǐhuan wǒ.

Dialogue Two

Wáng:	Xiǎo Lǐ, nǐ xǐ bu xǐhuan tī zúqiú?
Lǐ:	Bù xǐhuan, wǒ bú huì tī.
Wáng:	Nǐ xǐhuan dǎ wǎngqiú ma?
Lǐ:	Wǒ xǐhuan kàn, bù xǐhuan dǎ.
Wáng:	Wèishénme?
Lǐ:	Yīnwèi wǒ bú tài huì dǎ.
Wáng:	Wǒ yě bú tài huì, wǒmen yìqǐ xué, hǎo ma?
Lǐ:	Hǎo.

Reading

Nǐ Wǎnshang Dōu Zuò Shénme?

Nǐmen hǎo! Wǒ de Zhōngwén míngzi jiào Lǐ Dàmíng. Wǒ shì Fǎguórén, jīnnián shíjiǔ suì, shì Lúndūn Dàxué de xuésheng. Wǒ de zhuānyè shì Hànyǔ, wǒ yě xué Zhōngguó wénxué. Wǒ huì shuō Fǎyǔ, Yīngyǔ, Hànyǔ hé yìdiǎnr Rìyǔ. Wǒ xǐhuan xué wàiyǔ, yě hěn xǐhuan dǎ qiú. Wǒ xīngqīyī wǎnshang dǎ lánqiú, xīngqī'èr wǎnshang kàn Fǎwén shū, xīngqīsān wǎnshang dǎ wǎngqiú, xīngqīsì wǎnshang xué Zhōngwén, xīngqīwǔ wǎnshang tī zúqiú, xīngqīliù wǎnshang shàng wǎng kàn Zhōngguó diànyǐng, xīngqītiān wǎnshang wǒ xiě Hànzì. Nǐ wǎnshang dōu zuò shénme?

Lesson Seven Nǐmen Yǒu Běijīng Kǎoyā ma?

Dialogue One

Waiter:	Nǐmen hǎo! Nǐmen xiǎng hē diǎnr shénme?
Lǐ:	Yǒu méiyǒu Zhōngguó báijiǔ?
Waiter:	Duìbuqǐ, wǒmen zhǐ yǒu Zhōngguó hóngjiǔ.
Xiè:	Wǒmen jīntiān jiù hē hóngjiǔ ba.
Waiter:	Nǐmen yào jǐ píng?
Wáng:	Wǒmen zhǐ yǒu sì ge rén, xiān yào yì píng ba.
Waiter:	Hǎo. Nǐmen xiǎng chī diǎnr shénme?
Fāng:	Nǐmen yǒu Běijīng kǎoyā ma?
Waiter:	Yǒu. Wǒmen zhèr de Běijīng kǎoyā hěn yǒumíng.
Lǐ:	Nǐmen zhèr hái yǒu shénme hěn yǒumíng?
Waiter:	Wǒmen de hóngshāoròu yě hěn yǒumíng, hěn hǎochī.
Xiè:	Hǎo, wǒmen yào yí ge hóngshāoròu, yì zhī kǎoyā.
Wáng:	Zài diǎn yí ge chǎo qīngcài, yí ge niúròu chǎo báicài, sì wǎn chǎofàn.

Dialogue Two

Waiter:	Xiānsheng, nǐ xiǎng chī diǎnr shénme?
Lǐ:	Wǒ yào yì pán niúròu chǎofàn.
Waiter:	Hǎo. Nín xiǎng hē diǎnr shénme?
Lǐ:	Yǒu píjiǔ ma?
Waiter:	Yǒu. Yīngguó píjiǔ, Zhōngguó píjiǔ, wǒmen dōu yǒu.
Lǐ:	Yǒu méiyǒu Zhōngguó Wǔxīng Píjiǔ?
Waiter:	Yǒu.
Lǐ:	Tài hǎo le! Wǒ yào yì bēi Wǔxīng Píjiǔ.

Reading

Wǒ Xǐhuan Chī Zhōngguó fàn

Nǐmen hǎo! Nǐmen rènshi wǒ, wǒ shì Lǐ Dàmíng. Wǒ hěn xǐhuan chī Zhōngguó fàn, hē Zhōngguó chá. Wǒ tiāntiān hē Zhōngguó chá, kěshì wǒ hěn shǎo chī Zhōngguó fàn, yīnwèi wǒ bú huì zuò. Wǒ hěn xiǎng xué, kěshì méiyǒu lǎoshī. Wǒ de Zhōngwén lǎoshī yě bú huì zuò, tā shuō tā jiā tā xiānsheng zuò fàn, tā zhǐ huì chī, bú huì zuò. Shàngge xīngqīliù wǒmen lǎoshī jiā yǒu yí gè wǎnhuì. Wǎnhuì shang yǒu hěn duō hǎochī de fàncài. Zhōngguó cài yǒu Běijīng kǎoyā, hóngshāo niúròu, chǎofàn, hái yǒu chǎo qīngcài. Yīngguó cài yǒu kǎo niúròu hé sānmíngzhì. Yǒude rén chī Yīngguó fàn, yǒude rén chī Zhōngguó fàn, yǒude rén Yīngguó fàn, Zhōngguó fàn dōu chī, kěshì wǒ zhǐ chī Zhōngguó fàn, nǐmen yīnggāi zhīdào wèishénme.

Lesson Eight Wǒ Jiā Yǒu Sì Kǒu Rén

Dialogue One

Lǐ: Xiǎo Wáng, nǐ jiā yǒu jǐ kǒu rén?

Wáng: Wǒ jiā yǒu sì kǒu rén, bàba, māma, gēge hé wǒ.

Lǐ: Nǐ gēge yě shì xuésheng ma?

Wáng: Bù, tā shì yīshēng. Wǒ bàba, māma yě shì yīshēng.

Lǐ: Nǐ gēge de nǚ péngyou yě shì yīshēng ba?

Wáng: Tā hái méiyǒu nǚ péngyou ne. Nǐ bàba māma zuò shénme gōngzuò?

Lǐ: Wǒ bàba shì shāngrén, wǒ māma shì zuòjiā.

Wáng: Nǐmen jiā zhǐ yǒu sān kǒu rén ma?

Lǐ: Bù, wǒ hái yǒu yí ge jiějie, tā shì lǜshī.

Wáng: Wǒ jiā hái yǒu yì tiáo kě'ài de xiǎogǒu, nǐ jiā yǒu méiyǒu gǒu?

Lǐ: Wǒ jiā méiyǒu gǒu, wǒ mā bù xǐhuan gǒu, tā xǐhuan māo. Wǒ jiā yǒu liǎng zhī māo.

Dialogue Two

Lǐ: Xiǎo Wáng, nǐ jīntiān máng bu máng?

Wáng: Máng, wǒ jīntiān hěn máng. Nǐ ne?

Lǐ: Wǒ bú tài máng. Nǐ lèi bu lèi?

Wáng: Wǒ bú lèi, kěshì wǒ yǒudiǎnr kě.

Lǐ: Hē diǎnr chá ba, wǒ zhèr yǒu chá.

Wáng: Wǒ bú ài hē chá. Nǐ yǒu kāfēi ma?

Lǐ: Yǒu, nǐ è bu è? Wǒ zhèr hái yǒu chī de.

Wáng: Wǒ bú è, xièxie.

Lǐ: Bú kèqi.

Reading

Wǒ Jiā Yǒu Jǐ Kǒu Rén?

Wǒ jiào Fāng Míngyīng, jīnnián èrshí suì. Wǒ jiā yǒu bàba, māma, jiějie, mèimei hé wǒ. Wǒ bàba shì Yīngguórén, wǒ māma shì Zhōngguórén, tāmen dōu shì dàxué lǎoshī. Wǒ bàba shì Yīngwén lǎoshī, wǒ māma shì Zhōngwén lǎoshī. Wǒ jiějie shì lǜshī, tā de nán péngyou shì zuòjiā, tā shì Éluósīrén, tā huì shuō Yīngyǔ, Fǎyǔ, hé yìdiǎnr Hànyǔ, tā hěn xǐhuan xué wàiyǔ. Wǒ mèimei jīnnián bā suì, shì ge xiǎo xuésheng. Wǒmen jiā hái yǒu yì tiáo gǒu hé liǎng zhī māo. Wǒ mèimei shuō: " Wǒmen jiā yīnggāi shì jiǔ kǒu rén." Nǐ shuō wǒmen jiā yǒu jǐ kǒu rén?

Lesson Nine Běijīng Xiàtiān Bǐ Lúndūn Rè

Dialogue One

Fāng: Xiǎo Wáng, nà shì shuí? Shì nǐ nǚ péngyou ma?

Wáng:	Shì de. Tā jiào Qīngqing, hěn xǐhuan dǎ lánqiú.
Fāng:	Zhēn piàoliang! Tā gèzi hěn gāo.
Wáng:	Tā hé wǒ yíyàng gāo, wǒ yǒu diǎnr pàng.
Fāng:	Nǐ bú pàng, nǐ bǐ wǒ shòu duō le.
Wáng:	Nǐ yǒu méiyǒu nǚ péngyou?
Fāng:	Yǒu, wǒ nǚ péngyou shì Wáng Jīng de mèimei.
Wáng:	Shì ma? Tā bǐ nǐ xiǎo duō le ba?
Fāng:	Bù duō, tā zhǐ bǐ wǒ xiǎo sān suì.

Dialogue Two

Lǐ:	Xiǎo Wáng, Běijīng de tiānqì zěnmeyàng?
Wáng:	Xiàtiān hěn rè, dōngtiān hěn lěng.
Lǐ:	Běijīng xiàtiān bǐ Lúndūn rè ma?
Wáng:	Bǐ Lúndūn rè duō le!
Lǐ:	Shànghǎi ne?
Wáng:	Shànghǎi bǐ běijīng hái rè.
Lǐ:	Běijīng de chūntiān zěnmeyàng?
Wáng:	Chūntiān hěn hǎo, hěn nuǎnhuo. Kěshì méiyǒu Lúndūn nuǎnhuo.
Lǐ:	Chángcháng xià yǔ ma?
Wáng:	Chūntiān yǔ hěn shǎo, kěshì xiàtiān yǔ hěn duō.
Lǐ:	Běijīng dōngtiān xià bu xià yǔ?
Wáng:	Dōngtiān bú xià yǔ, dōngtiān xià xuě.
Lǐ:	Wǒ xǐhuan xià xuě tiān. Běijīng de qiūtiān zěnmeyàng?
Wáng:	Qiūtiān hěn hǎo, bù lěng bú rè.

Reading

Wǒ Jiějie hé Běijīng de Tiānqì

Wǒ jiějie jiào Lǐ Xiǎoyīng, tā shì lǜshī, tā zài Běijīng gōngzuò. Tā shuō tā hěn xǐhuan Běijīng de dōngtiān. Běijīng de dōngtiān hěn lěng, chángcháng xià xuě. Lúndūn de dōngtiān bǐ Běijīng nuǎnhuo, kěshì chángcháng xià yǔ, wǒ hé wǒ jiějie dōu bù xǐhuan xià yǔ tiān, wǒmen xǐhuan xià xuě tiān. Běijīng de xiàtiān hěn rè, bǐ Lúndūn rè duō le. Wǒ jiějie yǒu diǎnr pàng, tā bù xǐhuan tài rè de tiānqì, suǒyǐ tā bú tài xǐhuan Běijīng de xiàtiān. Běijīng de chūntiān hé qiūtiān hěn hǎo, bù lěng bú rè, yě bù chángcháng xià yǔ. Wǒ jiějie shuō, chūntiān de Běijīng hěn piàoliang, wǒ xiǎng míngnián chūntiān qù Běijīng kàn wǒ jiějie, yě kànkan piàoliang de Běijīng.

Lesson ten Nǐ Zěnme Qù Shāngdiàn?

Dialogue One

Wáng:	Xiǎo Lǐ, nǐ qù nǎr?
Lǐ:	Wǒ qù shāngdiàn.
Wáng:	Nǐ qù nǎ jiā shāngdiàn?
Lǐ:	Wǒ qù nà jiā Dōngfāng Shāngdiàn. Nǐ qù nǎr?
Wáng:	Wǒ qù túshūguǎn.
Lǐ:	Jīntiān xīngqīliù, nǐ qù túshūguǎn zuò shénme?

Wáng:	Wǒ qù túshūguǎn huán shū.
Lǐ:	Nǐ zěnme qù? Wǒ yǒu zìxíngchē, nǐ qí wǒ de chē qù ba.
Wáng:	Xièxie, wǒ xǐhuan zǒu lù, wǒ háishi zǒu lù qù ba.

Dialogue Two

Lǐ:	Lǎo Wáng, nǐ huí jiā ma?
Wáng:	Bù, wǒ xiān qù shāngxuéyuàn zài huí jiā.
Lǐ:	Nǐ qù shāngxuéyuàn zuò shénme?
Wáng:	Wǒ qù kàn yí ge péngyou. Tā shì nàr de lǎoshī.
Lǐ:	Míngtiān méiyǒu dìtiě, nǐ zěnme lái shàngbān?
Wáng:	Wǒ zuò huǒchē lái. Nǐ ne?
Lǐ:	Wǒ xiǎng zuò gōnggòng qìchē lái.
Wáng:	Nǐ zěnme bù dǎ dí lái? Dǎ dí bǐ zuò gōnggòng qìchē kuài duō le.
Lǐ:	Kěshì yě guì duō le.
Wáng:	Duì. Nǐ bú shì yǒu qìchē ma? Wèishénme bù kāi chē lái?
Lǐ:	Yīnwèi wǒ hái bú huì kāi chē.

Reading

Wǒ Xǐhuan Qí Chē Qù Shàngbān

Hěn duō rén xǐhuan kāi chē qù shàngbān, kěshì wǒ xǐhuan qí chē qù. Chūnxiàqiūdōng, wǒ chàbuduō tiāntiān dōu qí zìxíngchē qù shàngbān. Lúndūn méiyǒu dìtiě ma? Yǒu! Lúndūn de gōnggòng qìchē bù duō ma? Yǒu hěn duō! Kěshì wǒ jiù shì bù xǐhuan zuò. Lúndūn zuò dìtiě de rén hěn duō, xiàtiān zuò dìtiě hěn rè, zàishuō, zuò dìtiě yě hěn guì. Wǒ yě bù xǐhuan zuò Lúndūn de gōnggòng qìchē, Lúndūn lù shang de xíngrén hé qìchē tài duō, qí chē chángcháng bǐ zuò gōngòng qìchē hái kuài. Jīntiān shì xīngqīliù, wǒ bú shàngbān. Wǒ yào qí chē qù wǒ nǚ péngyou jiā, kàn tā bàba māma, wǎnshang wǒmen yìqǐ qù kàn diànyǐng.

Dr George X Zhang is the Director of the Language Centre and London Confucius Institute at the School of Oriental and African Studies, University of London. He has over twenty five years of experience working in British and Chinese universities with research interests and publications in language acquisition, cross cultural communications and teacher training. He was given a full professorship by the Shandong Normal University in 1994, made an honorary fellow by the Chartered Institute of Linguists in 2010, and is currently the coordinator of the European benchmarking Chinese language (EBCL) project.

Linda M Li is the principal lecturer in Chinese and the Deputy Head of the Department of Languages and Cross cultural Studies at Regents College, London. Linda has taught English and Chinese for over twenty years in secondary, tertiary and higher education institutions in China and the UK and has research interests in applied linguistics, social linguistics and language teaching for business purposes. She has also been actively involved in teacher education for the last five years.

Lik Suen is a senior lector of Chinese in the Department of China and Inner Asia at the School of Oriental and African Studies. She is a graduate of the Beijing Language Institute (now the Beijing Language and Culture University) with nearly 15 years' experience of teaching Chinese as a foreign language at universities in China's mainland , Hong Kong and London. She is studying for a PhD in applied linguistics at the University of London.